MULTI-SENSORY IDEAS FOR WORSHIP

Irene Smale is the Diocesan Children's Adviser for Chichester (UK). She has a Batchelor of Arts Degree in Theology and History as well as more than 36 years' experience in ministering to children and families in a team ministry alongside her husband Ish. To contact Irene or to find out more about their ministry you can email ishmael@ishmael.org.uk or visit their website at www.ishmaeldirect.com

Multi-Sensory Ideas for Worship

100 practical activities for children's and family ministry

IRENE SMALE

with songs by Ishmael

David C Cook

First published 2009
Published by David C. Cook
Kingsway Communications Ltd
26–28 Lottbridge Drove, Eastbourne BN23 6NT, UK

David C. Cook
4050 Lee Vance View, Colorado Springs, CO 80918, USA

David C. Cook Distribution Canada
55 Woodslee Avenue, Paris, Ontario, Canada N3L 3E5

ISBN 978 1 84291392 5

Cover design by PinnacleCreative.co.uk

1 2 3 4 5 6 printing 12 11 10 09
Printed in Italy

Contents

HEAR

TOUCH

Introduction

To dwell in the presence of God.
To listen to His voice.
To look at His beauty
To touch God's incarnate Word.
To taste fully God's infinite goodness.[1]

A Biblical Approach

I first encountered a multi-sensory approach to education in Bible times, when researching for my book *A History of Children: From the Ancient World to Jesus Christ.*[2] On his first day at synagogue school, a five year old Jewish boy would be welcomed by his teacher, a rabbi, and shown a large slate or rock. On it would be carved the letters of the Hebrew alphabet in various combinations. There would also be two of the basic texts of the Law: Leviticus 1:1, "The Lord called to Moses and spoke to him from the Tent of Meeting" and Deuteronomy 33:4, "The law that Moses gave us, the possession of the assembly of Jacob". In addition to these one other sentence was inscribed, "The Law will be my calling." The teacher read these words out to the boy and the boy would repeat them back. The slate was then smeared with honey, and the boy was allowed to trace the letters with his fingers in the honey and lick them afterwards. He was then reminded of Ezekiel, who said after eating the scroll, "I ate it; and it tasted

[1] Nouwen, Henri (1989). *In The Name of Jesus.* London: Darton, Longman & Todd. p. 29
[2] Smale, Irene E. (1998). *A History of Children.* London: Silver Fish Publishing. p. 143

as sweet as honey in my mouth."[3] After this ceremony the boy was given sweet honey cakes to eat, shaped in the letters of the Hebrew alphabet.

There are of course numerous references to honey in the Scriptures, for example Psalm 119:103: "How sweet are your words to my taste, sweeter than honey to my mouth!" The ancient Jews believed that learning should be a sweet, enjoyable and rewarding experience. So all of the senses were employed in the learning process: seeing and reading the scriptures, hearing them and repeating them back, touching the carved out shapes of the letters and smelling and tasting the sweetness of the honey as the letters were traced by the boy. What a lovely way to learn scripture and to worship God!

The method that was used over 2000 years ago is still vital in the learning process today. The practice of involving as many of the senses as possible in the teaching method is often referred to as a multi-sensory approach. Not only is it the most natural way to learn and a lot of fun for children and adults, it really works. The human brain obtains and interprets information more readily when the senses are stimulated. We make important connections and understand concepts more easily when the learning experience involves sight, smell, sound, taste and touch.

Educational Theory

Research has shown that multi-sensory techniques are the most effective way to teach, because multi-sensory instruction encourages action and interaction. It's the perfect approach for the majority of children who enjoy learning by doing. The more the senses are employed, the more children enjoy learning.

It has only been since the Industrial Revolution in the nineteenth century that the more formal approach to learning using only two of the senses, of seeing and hearing, became a restrictive practice in the classroom. Prior to that, learning was very much an apprentice or 'hands-on' approach. Nowadays the multi-sensory method is used in a vast number of educational contexts.

Maria Montessori (1870–1952) the Italian physician, educator, philosopher, humanitarian and devout Catholic helped to introduce the multi-sensory method of learning. She taught children from birth through to adolescence. Each subject area in a Montessori school integrates the senses. She believed the use of music, art and exposure to beautiful surroundings would enhance the learning experience.[4]

---

[3] Ezekiel 3:3

[4] Montessori, M. (1967). *The Absorbent Mind.* (C. A. Claremont, Trans.). New York: Holt, Rinehart and Winston.

Around the same time as Montessori, Dr Samuel Orton (1879–1948) an American physician was pioneering studies in learning disabilities and dyslexia. Dr Orton integrated kinaesthetic and tactile learning strategies with the teaching of visual and auditory concepts. He was influenced by the work of fellow educational psychologist Fernald.

Grace Fernald (1879–1950) established the first clinic for remedial instruction in 1921 at the University of California. Tracing tactile learning methods back to Quintilian (c.35–96 A.D.) Seguin (1812–1880) and Montessori, Fernald's kinaesthetic spelling and reading practice involved writing in the air and tracing words in large written or scripted format, while simultaneously saying the names and sounds of the letters. Her theory incorporates the physical with the auditory, verbal and visual elements of reading and is known as VAKT (visual, auditory, kinaesthetic, tactile).

Later Orton worked with Anna Gillingham who introduced a systematic approach for teaching letters using sounds. Their combined theory has become known as the Orton-Gillingham teaching method and is one of the basic forms of remediation tutoring for children with dyslexia.[5]

More recently Don Campbell's controversial book[6] discusses the theory that listening to Mozart may temporarily increase the IQ and produce many other beneficial effects on the mind. Campbell's sequel, *The Mozart Effect For Children*[7] argues that music can improve listening disorders e.g. dyslexia, attention deficit disorder and autism. The popular impact of the Mozart effect was demonstrated in 1998 when the governor of Georgia announced a state budget proposal to include a CD of classical music for every child born in Georgia.

Educational Practice

Educationalists and parents acknowledge that children are exceptionally sensitive to their environment. Their condition affects their mood. Young children are not content to simply look at an object and say they understand it. They are compelled to examine it with all of their senses. It was the Swiss developmental psychologist Jean Piaget (1896–1980) in his systematic study of the understanding in children

---

[5] Orton, S.T. (1937). *Reading, Writing and Speech Problems In Children: A presentation of certain types of disorders in the development of the language faculty*. New York: W. W. Norton.

[6] Campbell, D. (1997) *The Mozart Effect: Tapping the Power of Music to Heal the Body, Strengthen the Mind, and Unlock the Creative Spirit*, New York, Harper Collins.

[7] Campbell, D. (2000) *The Mozart Effect For Children: Awakening your child's mind, health, and creativity with music.* New York: Harper Collins.

who saw children as 'Little Scientists' making and testing hypotheses to understand their world.[8]

Scholars of the theory and practice of play remind us that from birth we are continually investigating our environment and gathering information through our senses. Early childhood educators encourage young children to finger-paint, cut paper, and work with sand, glue and scented clay in order to engage their senses in the learning process. There are currently thousands of educational resources that offer suggestions for learning activities and play related to the multi-sensory method.

The language arts such as prose, poetry and plays all naturally invoke our senses. The authors of children's illustrated literature use descriptive language and images that invite us to listen, look, touch, smell and taste their stories. We also have available wonderfully illustrated guides for understanding the Bible and learning about the manners and customs of the period. And of course in today's virtual world of information technology we can interact and engage our senses through computer simulations.

So What Has This To Do With Worship?

The word 'worship' is derived from the Old English *weorthscipe* translated as worth + ship and means: to show profound religious devotion and respect; adore or venerate. In the Old Testament there are many instances of individual worship.[9] There are times when the patriarchs like Abraham worshipped the Lord wherever he spontaneously chose to appear to them. There are also many instances of collective worship.[10] Ritual was a distinctive characteristic of Tabernacle and Temple worship. As well as the daily morning and evening sacrifices, the various festivals including the Passover and the Day of Atonement would be focal points in the Jewish calendar.

When the Temple was destroyed and the exiles found themselves in Babylon they had to adapt and create a new way to worship. The home became a *miqdash me'at* meaning a small sanctuary.[11] Wherever they dwelt, they prayed, recited scriptures, studied, lit oil lamps, sang songs, and ate together as a worshipping community. Later the synagogue service consisted of the *Shema* (Jewish Creed),

---

8 Piaget, Jean (1932). *The Moral Judgement of the Child.* London: Routledge and Kegan Paul.

9 e.g. Gen 24:6; Ex 34:8

10 e.g. Ps 42:4; 1 Chron 29:20

11 Smale, Irene E. *A History of Children.* p. 156

prayers, scripture readings, and exposition. After the construction of the second temple, the daily services, the Sabbath, the annual festivals and fasts and the praises of the Hymn Book (Book of Psalms) ensured that worship remained integral to Jewish life.

In the New Testament we read that Jesus participated in both private and collective worship, but he always emphasised that worship must be the love from our heart towards our heavenly Father. Worship is the life of an individual person, offered to God, not only in the sense of individual and collective worship but also in service to each other and all of humanity.[12]

As the Early Church began to develop Christians didn't abandon Temple worship immediately but continued to attend the synagogue services. When the break between Judaism and Christianity finally came, Church worship may have been modelled on the synagogue service. Any detailed description of Christian worship during this period appears vague. We read in Acts 20:7 that the day of worship was the first day of the week, Sunday, although Acts 2:46 tells us that they also met daily. Worship was conducted in believers' homes. Simplicity was the key to house church worship services, consisting mostly of: praise[13], prayer, readings from the scriptures and exposition. The Love Feast, followed by the Lord's Supper,[14] was integral to Christian worship and the emphasis was on the Holy Spirit, love and devotion to God.

For Christians, worship is at the heart of our life as a community of faith. In our worship we give honour and praise to God and we are also drawn into the mystery of God and into a deeper relationship with Him. Through words, music, silence, symbols, movement, ritual, prayer, preaching, and the creative combination of these elements – we are called to engage our hearts, minds, senses and imagination in the love of God. This is made visible in Jesus Christ and experienced in the life and power of the Holy Spirit.

What Is Multi-Sensory Worship?

At the beginning of this introduction I explained a method of education in Bible times that incorporated the senses. Worship in the Old Testament and the Early Church

---

[12] Mt 5:23; Lk 10:27; Jn 4:23; Jas 1:27

[13] Eph 5:19; Col 3:16

[14] The "love feast" was a full meal, with each participant bringing food to share and be eaten in a common room. It was held on a Sunday, which became known as the Lord's Day with reference to the resurrection, the appearance of Christ to the disciples on the road to Emmaus, the appearance

was very much a "multi-sensory" experience. Throughout history the Church has been known as the centre of visual arts. The masterpieces of Michelangelo, Da Vinci, Raphael and Rembrandt, etc, were part of the visual fabric of worship. Brilliantly coloured stained glass windows told the story of Jesus' life and death. Bells were rung and incense burned as music was performed by perfectly pitched and elaborately robed choirs, to enrich the worship experience and exalt God. The high point was the Mass in which the one holy catholic and apostolic Church shared the bread and the wine, celebrating Christ's body and blood which was sacrificed for all mankind. In a knee-jerk reaction to this form of ritual, the Church appears to have lost her multi-sensory heritage. Services have been reduced to a worship experience using only the one auditory sense i.e. listening to a singer, a keyboard, a band or maybe a choir and a minister preaching from a platform. Boring for children and very often for adults as well!

Multi-sensory worship brings together the practice of using the senses combined with the depth of spirituality in Christian liturgy, ritual and scripture and is accessible to all ages. This is not a new concept. More recently innovations such as Sacred Space, Labyrinths, Critical Mass, Godly Play, Messy Church and Fresh Expressions have helped the Church to explore further notions of interactive worship. There are thousands of ideas incorporating multi-sensory worship today. These usually involve a plethora of activities or prayer stations that evoke all of the senses, as opposed to just singing songs, listening to a sermon and saying prayers. They involve the whole body in worship.

Multi-sensory worship uses a diversity of music styles including anything from Gregorian plainsong to ethereal digital sounds, to inspire and create the worship environment. The audio-visual screen acts as the stained glass window of the twenty-first century. The use of Scripture together with information technology, lighting effects, multi-media, drama, narration, meditative readings, imagery, ancient and extemporaneous prayers offers interaction. Similarly working Scripture and liturgy together with raw materials, stone, clay, fabric, water, earth, paint, wood, candles, the smell of fresh flowers and baking bread incorporates all of the senses into the worship experience. Multi-sensory worship allows us to rediscover some of the Church's rich liturgical and ritual heritage and helps us to communicate the scriptures in a way that transcends linguistic and cultural barriers. By employing all of the five senses in collective and individual worship, we actually 'do' worship.

---

to Thomas and Pentecost. All these took place on Sundays after the Passion. Following the meal was a re-enactment of the Last Supper, where the words of the institution were prayed over the bread and wine which was then shared by all the faithful present. 1 Cor. 11:23–26.

Interactive prayer and worship installations are adaptable and can be set around a nave, church hall, school room or into any space. They can be a useful aid to worship for all ages. A 'see' station might include paintings, prints or imagery to help focus on a particular theme. A 'touch' station might make available a tray of sand or earth, fabric and other materials such as paint and clay. A supervised open space specifically for movement can also be helpful, e.g. an area where more physically active children can move around, pace or dance. A 'hear' station might involve music CDs, authors and poets reading aloud or for children to listen while drawing or writing. The 'smell' station could incorporate scented oils, candles, flowers and freshly baked bread. A 'taste' station can be easily set up in a way that is non-allergenic and food health and hygiene conscious. A quiet area under a softly-lit canvas gazebo with rugs, cushions and pens and paper for drawing and writing can have a calming effect as an aid to listening and also serve as a prayer space for individuals, families and groups at peer level.

Stations or activities are not difficult to set up, they need not be expensive, they allow creative use of the imagination, they are adaptable for all ages and enhance the worship experience.

Using this book

This book is simply a springboard of 100 ideas to launch you into being more creative by engaging all ages and abilities in multi-sensory worship. I offer 20 ideas for each of the five senses. Each idea is based on a Bible verse, and there is a different prayer and a corresponding song related to each theme. Each idea has two options: the first is more appropriate for groups where there is a period of activity – maybe a children's Sunday group or a youth club or an all-age service where you include a time for craft or group interaction; the second is more appropriate for a traditional style service where seats are fixed in rows and there isn't an opportunity for interaction, but you may adapt the ideas to fit your situation.

The following symbols are used to help you identify the components of each idea:

Bible reference

Equipment you may need to collect in advance

An art or craft option

A puzzle, quiz or game option

An active game or activity option

The option for a more traditional style service

Prayer

Song

The ideas are grouped by sense and there is a scripture reference index at the back.

Many of the ideas are based on ancient Bible manners and customs and have been tried and tested mostly within the context of all age worship services and workshops that I have led over the past few years.

The songs are all written and recorded by my husband Ishmael or Ish as he is affectionately known. We have worked together in many countries and contexts as a team ministry for over 36 years with families and children. For more information about our ministry please visit www.ishmaeldirect.com. Ish has recorded and produced over 40 albums. He has written songs to enhance the worship of an individual or group and many of his songs are simply scripture verses set to popular music that can be easily learned off by heart. This, we discovered, was of course, another biblical approach to learning Scripture. In Bible times this was achieved very often through the rhythmic chanting of texts as an aid to memory. For information on where you can find recordings, downloads and sheet music for the songs please visit our website.

I hope you enjoy the ideas in this book and have fun with them. My prayer is that you may be inspired to worship as I have been, through the gifts of creativity and imagination that God has generously bestowed on us all. We who are created in the image of 'the Creator God' are invited in turn to become the inspirers and creators.

Irene Smale

SEE

A SHINING LIGHT

Matthew 5:16

Let your light shine before men, that they may see your good deeds and praise your Father in heaven.

Clear glass jars; acetate marker pens; tea lights or small candles; lighting tapers; trays; glow sticks.

The sun gives us light by day and the moon and stars light up the night. Light makes us feel safe. Decorate jars with the acetate pens, with patterns and the prayer. Place a tea light in each jar. The Bible says Christians are to be shining lights that show God's love in a dark world. People will be attracted by the light, experience the safety of God's love, and praise Him. Light the tea lights and give out glow sticks to be waved as the song is sung.

Give everyone a tea light or candle as they arrive. Either place trays on a table at the front; invite several people to bring their tea lights to the trays, light them with tapers, and stay; repeat until all the tea lights are lit and everyone is at the front, or light one candle at the end of each row of seats and ask people to carefully light the candle next to them until all are lit. The Bible says Christians are to be lights shining in a dark world. People will come from the darkness, drawn by the safety and warmth of God's love, and praise him. Turn all other lights off and pray the prayer below.

Dear Lord, please help me to shine and spread your light to all around me. Amen.

You never put a light under a dirty old bucket
You never put a light under a dirty old bucket
You never put a light under a dirty old bucket
If you want light to shine around, round, round

Shine, shine around, round, round
Shine, shine around, round, round
Shine a light that everyone can see, see, see

Lord help me let my little light shine
Not just Sundays all the time
So friends give praise to you when they see me.

Ian Smale

IDEA 2

AN OFFERING TO GOD

1 Kings 18:32
With the stones he built an altar in the name of the Lord.

Clean, smooth stones, large enough to write on; marker or felt pens.

In Bible times people built a mound, or cairn, made of stones in special places to worship God and make an offering to Him. Choose a stone and write a word or draw a shape that represents what you want to offer to God e.g. a worry, a skill or hobby, your love, plans, etc. Now offer it to God by kneeling down and placing the stone with others in a mound. When everyone has piled their stones on the cairn, repeat the prayer below line by line.

In Old Testament times those who wanted to offer worship to God often built a cairn of stones. Quietly build a small cairn of stones and display the written prayer next to it. Invite people to choose a stone and write on it what they are offering to God. They can add their stones to the cairn, praying the prayer as they do so.

Heavenly Father, I give over to you today (name your offering).
I place it into your hands to do with what you will. Amen.

I'll sing to you
I'll bring to you
My life just like
An offering
I'll sing to you
I'll bring to you
My life of praise.

Ian Smale

BAPTISM

Matthew 3:16

As soon as Jesus was baptised, he went up out of the water. At that moment heaven was opened, and he saw the Spirit of God descending like a dove and lighting on him. And a voice from heaven said, "This is my Son, whom I love; with him I am well pleased."

Outlines of a dove on sheets of paper (use the template below); pens; scissors; purple and grey wax crayons; garden cane; cotton.

Give everyone a dove outline to cut out. Think of words that tell how you could be more like Jesus e.g. kind, gentle, loving, obedient. Write them on the dove with different coloured pens. Lightly shade the dove with the purple and grey wax crayons. You could make a dove mobile with several prayers suspended from a cane or a metal coat hanger using cotton.

Invite everyone to suggest ways to please God more. Each idea can be written on a dove. If someone is being baptised then a prayer for that person can also be written on the dove. Attach the doves to canes with the cotton. Have helpers hold the cane(s) up high between them and gently flutter the doves while the prayer is prayed and the song is sung.

Dear Lord,
I want to be more like you and live to please you.
I need your help.
Amen.

Take my life Lord
Make my life Lord
More like yours Lord, every day.
I just want to live to please You
To be like you in every way.
So take my life Lord,
Make my life Lord
More like yours Lord, every day.

Ian Smale

CREATURES

Genesis 2:20

So the man gave names to all the livestock, the birds of the air and all the beasts of the field.

Wildlife magazines; stickers; frieze paper; glue; scissors; pens; PowerPoint display.

Find as many different pictures of creatures as you can. Divide the frieze into different habitats e.g. rainforest, polar, desert, forest, sea, sky; or creature types e.g. mammals, fish, birds, reptiles, insects; or if you have mainly younger children, wild and domestic animals. Pictures can be cut or torn out and stuck on the paper in the appropriate sections.

Show a PowerPoint display of a wide range of different creatures. Ask volunteers to identify each creature and pray the prayer.

As you pick up or view each picture thank God for making that particular amazing creature. Let's also pray we take good care of the animals God has created for us to enjoy.

In the sea, in the sea
God knows every fish
That swims in every sea
All the fish, God can see
But I know he's got
A special love for you and me

On the land, on the land
God knows every beast
That lives in every land
But I know he's got
A special love for you and me

In the sky, in the sky
God knows every bird
That flies high in the sky
All the birds, God can see
But I know he's got
A special love for you and me.

Ian Smale

DREAMS

Ecclesiastes 5:7

Much dreaming and many words are meaningless. Therefore stand in awe of God.

Paper; thin card; glue; pens; scissors.

Draw a simple cloud shape and photocopy one outline for each person. Many people ‘see’ dreams in their sleep. Sometimes we say ‘sweet dreams’ just before we go to bed. Cut out the cloud shape and stick it onto a piece of card. Draw a picture in the cloud shape of what a ‘sweet dream’ might be. Around the cloud draw and name pictures of some Bible people who talked about their dreams. You can keep the picture near your bed to remind you to pray the prayer below at bedtime.

Randomly stick photocopied clouds onto a large piece of paper or card. Invite volunteers to come and draw a picture in a cloud of their idea of a ‘sweet dream’. Has anyone ever heard from God in a dream, like in Bible times? Write around the clouds the names of Bible people who talked about their dreams.

Cut out thirteen extra clouds and write a word of the prayer on each one. Fix them to the floor, leading from the frieze to your seating area. As people return to their seats they can step on each one, saying the prayer aloud.

Lord, please help me to have sweet dreams and not bad ones. Amen

No matter how much you dream
How much useless work you do
Or how much you talk
You must still stand, stand, stand
In awe of God.

Ian Smale

IDEA 6

FAMILY

Galatians 6:10

Let us do good to all people, especially to those who belong to the family of believers.

Very simple people shapes in three sizes to represent adults, older children & teens and younger children; pens; staplers or sticky tape.

Photocopy the different sized paper people. Families come in all shapes and sizes. We are all part of the family of the church. What a huge family! All joined together with love. Each person chooses paper people to represent their family unit. They could cut them out, colour them in and write the names on each paper person. Join all the paper people together in a long chain. Invite everyone to stand in one large circle round the room holding the people paper chain. Pray out loud together.

Cut out lots of each of the different sizes of paper people. Either hand them round to everyone and ask them to write the names of their family on the appropriate people and then collect them all back, or take a quick count of your congregation, multiply by 4 (to estimate the family not present, e.g. parents, grandparents, children, grandchildren, siblings etc) and then ask for volunteers to come and join up all the paper people in a long chain (this could be done during a time of singing or teaching). Hold up the chain of people and pray together.

Thank you God for my family and the family of the church. Amen.

Through faith in Christ we now can be
Children in God's family
Through faith in Christ we now can be
Children in God's family

Family, family, me and you, you and me
Family, family, children in God's family

His sons and daughters we can be
Children in God's family

We are so thankful we can be
Children in God's family.

We now can be in God's family.
We now can be in God's family.
We now can be in God's family.

Ian Smale

FIRM FOUNDATIONS

Matthew 7:24

Therefore everyone who hears these words of mine and puts them into practice is like a wise man who built his house on the rock.

Card, board or canvas; paints; brushes; water; stones or coloured pebbles; glue.

Jesus said that if we listen to him then we will be like the wise man in his story who built his house well. Paint a picture of your house onto card, board or canvas. Glue a frame of different-coloured small stones or pebbles around the edge. As you glue each stone pray the prayer below.

Remind everyone that the reason Jesus told his story was so that we would listen to him and build our lives on a solid foundation. Display a large picture of a house painted on card, board or canvas. Invite people to pick up a stone and pray the prayer below as they add it to a pile at the base of the picture.

Lord please help me always to listen to your voice and to build my life on your solid foundation. Amen.

There was a little man and he had a little house
Somewhere near the gentle rolling sea.
He found a little site that he thought would suit him well
A perfect place to build security.
Well the sand was level and the sand was flat
With a saw and a chisel and a rat-a-tat
With a bucket full of this and a shovel full of that
His house was very soon built.

"What a house look come and see!"
He said to all he knew;
"This house will last as long as me!"
And sadly that was true.

All was fine and rosy till the winter came along
Then suddenly the gentle rolling sea
Became a little rough, and the winds began to blow
It began to smash his little property
For the winds went whoosh, and his house went splat
Just like a pancake it was flat.
The wind and the rain had seen about that
There's now no house at all.

Another little man built another little house
Somewhere near the gentle rolling sea.
He found a little site that he thought would suit him well,
A perfect place to build security.
Well, the rock was level and the rock was flat,
With a saw and a chisel and a rat-a-tat;
With a bucket full of this and a shovel full of that,
His house was very soon built.

"What a house, look come and see!"
I've built on rock – it's stronger;
This house will last as long as me,
Forever, if not longer."

All was fine and rosy till the winter came along,
Then suddenly the gentle rolling sea
Became a little rough, and the winds began to blow,
But it couldn't harm his little property.
For the winds went whoosh, but his house stood good,
It stood as firm as a Christmas pud.
The wind and rains blew as hard as they could,
But his house, it would not budge.

Ian Smale

GOD'S PLANS

Jeremiah 29:11–13

"For I know the plans I have for you," declares the Lord, "plans to prosper you and not to harm you, plans to give you hope and a future. Then you will call upon me and come and pray to me, and I will listen to you. You will seek me and find me when you seek me with all your heart."

Large sheets of plain paper; green, orange and yellow paper; pens; glue; scissors; PowerPoint display.

God's people were taken far from home to another country. They were very sad. Jeremiah told them God had good plans for them. They were to build houses and settle their families in Babylon. One day God would rescue them and bring them home again to their own country. God has good plans for families. Draw and photocopy simple leaf shapes and encourage everyone to build a basic family tree, writing names or drawing family members, one per leaf and sticking them onto an outline trunk drawn on a large sheet of paper. Looking at all the family trees, pray the prayer together.

God's people in exile in Babylon felt far from home and far from God. They didn't believe they could settle but Jeremiah told them of God's good plans for them, even in Babylon. God promised to eventually deliver them and take them home. God has good plans for families. Show a display of pictures of different family groups (it would be best if they can be families from your own church). Intersperse the pictures of families with pictures of trees. Encourage personal reflection on God's plans for family members, the family unit and the family of God, the church.

Dear God, thank you that you have a plan and a purpose for me and my family.

Please help me to remember that you only want the best for me. Amen.

God has got plans for us
God plans success for us
God's plans will not harm us
His plans will give us hope
And a future
And the Lord will fulfil
His purpose for me
Fulfil his purpose in me.

God won't forget our work
God won't forget our love
God won't forget
We've helped his people
As we show our love for him

Ian Smale

LIGHT

Matthew 5:14
You are the light of the world.

Large world map; lantern; clear glass jars; tea-lights; lighting tapers; PowerPoint display.

Place a large world map on the floor. Point out your own country. Long ago, people from far away brought the good news of Jesus to our country. Trace out the journey from Jerusalem to your town. The message of Jesus brings light, love and hope. Invite people to identify regions where there is famine, natural disaster or war and place lighted tea-light candles in jars on those areas of the map. We can ask Jesus to use us to take the message of his light, love and hope to people in difficult situations and change lives. Pray the prayer below. (Children must be supervised at all times when using candles.)

Display a map of the world. Put a tea-light candle in a storm lantern. If your church has workers in a region where there is famine, natural disaster or war, overlay a visual of a candle or lamp on the map, or point it out on screen and put the lantern on a central table. Invite observations on the difficulties people face there. Encourage everyone to consider practical ways to help. Light the candle with the taper and pray.

Pray for the leaders of the regions you have identified.
Pray for the people who are suffering.
Pray for church workers there.
Pray for Jesus, the light of the world, to shine and bring his peace

I'm like a little light a-shining in the dark
I'm like a little light shining all around
And the light of my life is the Lord Jesus Christ
He's the brightest light that ever can be found
So, if you are living in the dark
If it seems there is darkness all around
Let the Lord Jesus Christ be the light of your life
'Cos He's the brightest light that ever can be found

Ian Smale

IDEA 10

LOVE

1 John 4:7
Dear friends, let us love one another, for love comes from God.

Pink or red A4 sheets of coloured paper; scissors; pens; glue.

On each sheet of paper, draw two identical heart shapes per person. On the first heart each person draws a picture of him/herself. On the other heart they draw a picture of someone they would like Jesus to bless. On the back of the second heart shape write the words, 'I know Jesus loves ....' and put their name. Now glue the two hearts together, back to back. Encourage everyone in turn to pray the prayer. Take your heart shape home. Where will you keep it to remind you to keep asking Jesus to bless the person on your heart?

Give out a heart shape to each person. They can write the name or draw a picture of someone they want to pray for. Display the prayer below on a screen so that people can personalise their prayer. Ask them to wave their heart in the air as everyone prays aloud together. Remind them to continue praying.

Lord, please bless (name of person) and help them get to know you better. Amen.

I know Jesus loves me
I know Jesus loves me
I know Jesus loves me
I know Jesus loves me
I know he loves little ones
As much as he loves Dads and Mums
Yes I know Jesus loves me
And I know he loves you too.

Ian Smale

IDEA 11

MY HEART

Psalm 119:11
I have hidden your word in my heart that I might not sin against you.

Origami or thin coloured paper; paper; scissors; pens.

Make an origami heart or paper heart shape with a slit opening down the middle (using instructions that can be found easily through searching on the internet). Write out the Bible verse above on a smaller heart shape, choosing two colours to write alternate letters. Now tuck the verse into the opening in the larger heart. Reading the Bible helps us to live God's way and reminds us to stop doing wrong things. Where will you keep your paper heart at home to remind you to do what it says?

Practise until you are confident you can make an origami heart. Either give a piece of paper to each person or invite volunteers to come to the front. Get everyone to follow your example and make a heart. Hand out slips of paper with the Bible verse photocopied onto them and invite people to tuck it into their origami heart. Encourage everyone to devise a plan to read more of God's Word. Discuss with a friend how you might achieve this. They may even offer support and help to motivate you to keep going. The prayer can be prayed with a friend.

Dear Lord, please help me always to keep your word in my heart. Amen.

Lord give me a heart that's true
Help me keep loving you
Watch over all I do
This is my prayer.

Be in my thoughts today
Help me in what I say
But most of all I pray
Make me like you.

Ian Smale

MY JOURNEY

Genesis 12:1–3

The Lord said to Abram, "Leave your country, your people and your father's household and go to the land I will show you. I will make you into a great nation and I will bless you; I will make your name great, and you will be a blessing. I will bless those who bless you, and whoever curses you I will curse; and all peoples on earth will be blessed through you."

A book of mazes or search for printable maze puzzles on the web; pens; flipchart.

God had a special purpose for Abram and told him when and where to move so that Abram would be in the right place at the right time. Photocopy maze puzzles of appropriate levels of difficulty for everyone. God has good purposes for your life. He will lead you and you can trust him as you follow in his way.

The Bible is full of stories about how God led his people. These stories teach us about the past and help build up faith for our own journey. Invite everyone to consider their own life story and how God has led them so far. Write on the flipchart significant or special events where God's leading was clear. Display the prayer and ask everyone to pray reflectively.

Thank you God, for all the things that have happened in my life.

Please help me to be a blessing to others as I continue my journey of faith with you. Amen.

So I've made up my mind
That I'm gonna follow him
Wherever Jesus leads me I will go

I may be scared by the things I see
But Jesus won't let them destroy me

I may be scared by the things I hear
But Jesus won't let me live in fear

I may be scare by the things I know
But Jesus won't ever let me go.

Ian Smale

PRAYER ART

1 Kings 6:29

On the walls all round the temple, in both the inner and outer rooms, he carved cherubim, palm trees and open flowers.

Paper; paints; brushes; water; wax crayons; felt pens; PowerPoint display.

When words are hard to find, or seem inadequate, you can paint or draw your prayers instead. Think about how great God is to create our beautiful world, with things seen and unseen. Use the paints or crayons to paint or draw the picture that comes into your mind.

Engage people in the prayer by showing a slideshow of appropriate photographs or works of art that illustrate the wonder of God's creation, some overwritten by lines of the prayer.

Dear Lord, thank you that you have created me in your image.

Please help me to appreciate the beautiful world you have created around me. Amen.

In the beginning God created the heavens and the earth
On day one God made light
Light and God was pleased with all he made

On day two sea and sky
Sea and sky, light and God
Was pleased with all he made

On day three land, plants, seeds
Land, plants, seeds
Sea and sky, light and God
Was pleased with all he made

On day four sun, moon, stars
Sun, moon, stars
Land, plants, seeds
Sea and sky, light and God
Was pleased with all he made

On day five fish and birds
Fish and birds
Sun, moon, stars
Land, plants, seeds
Sea and sky, light and God
Was pleased with all he made

On day six animals, humans
Animals, humans,
Fish and birds
Sun, moon, stars
Land, plants, seeds
Sea and sky, light and God
Was pleased with all he made

On day seven God took a rest
After making......

Ian Smale

PRAYER SCROLLS

Luke 4:17–20

The scroll of the prophet Isaiah was handed to him. Unrolling it, he found the place where it is written: "The Spirit of the Lord is upon me, because he has anointed me to preach good news to the poor. He has sent me to proclaim freedom for the prisoners and recovery of sight for the blind, to release the oppressed, to proclaim the year of the Lord's favour."

Cream paper, parchment or white paper steeped in cold tea and dried; sticky tape; pens; scissors; string or ribbon; picture of Jesus in the synagogue.

In Bible times books were written on rolls of papyrus or skins, called scrolls. All the Bible scrolls were kept in a precious box. Look up Luke 4:17. Try to find a picture illustrating this verse. Join several sheets of paper together, making long, narrow strips. Help everyone to choose a verse to copy (e.g. Psalm 47:1–2) onto the scroll. Show how to roll the scroll up from both ends and tie with ribbon. If you have time, people could make several scrolls and keep them in a decorated shoebox. Each day they could choose a different scroll to unroll and read. Pass around a scroll with a Bible verse as you pray.

In Bible times God's Word was written on rolls of papyrus made from reeds or skins. The scrolls were rolled up and kept in a special box. God's Word was honoured and revered. Provide lengths of paper or parchment and invite volunteers to come and write a favourite Bible verse on a scroll which they can roll up, tie with ribbon and place in a box. Families might like to make a box at home and put in it small rolls of paper containing some of God's promises. They can choose a different one to unroll and say each day.

Heavenly Father, please help me to read and understand your word so I can get to know you better. Amen.

I have got a special book
The Bible is its name
I've got lots of other books
But none are quite the same
The more I read my special book
The more I look and see
The God above is God of love
Who loves a child like me.

Ian Smale

SORRY STONES

1 John 1:9

If we confess our sins, he is faithful and just and will forgive us our sins and purify us from all unrighteousness.

Smooth stones; pencils or washable felt pens; soapy water and bowl; kitchen roll; baskets.

Make Sorry Stones:

- Choose a stone and with a pencil write on it something you want to say sorry to God for.
- Now wash the stone in the soapy water and dry it.

Take the Sorry Stone home as a reminder that God can wash away our sins and forgive us when we are sorry for doing wrong.

Display the prayer. Offer everyone a Sorry Stone from a basket and invite them to write with a pencil something they are truly sorry for. Give time for reflection on positive steps to take next time when they are tempted to think or do something they know is wrong. As people are invited to the front to wash their Sorry Stone in the soapy water as a symbol of God's forgiveness, encourage them to find a prominent place at home for the stone as a reminder of God's forgiveness and mercy.

Heavenly Father, thank you that you forgive me for the wrong things I do. Please help me to forgive others. Amen.

Every time we confess our sins
He is faithful and just and forgives us (x 2)

Jesus makes us clean inside
Jesus makes us clean inside
All the wrongs we could not hide
Have been made right when Jesus died.

You are kind and forgiving, O Lord,
Abounding in love to all who call. (x 2)

As far as the east is from the west
So far has he removed our sins from us (x 2)

Ian Smale

STORMS OF LIFE

Matthew 8:27

The men were amazed and asked, "What kind of man is this? Even the winds and the waves obey him!"

Sheets of A3 paper; pens; PowerPoint display.

When Jesus and his friends were in a boat on the lake, there was a huge, frightening storm. Jesus miraculously calmed the storm. His friends were amazed. There are times when things seem really bad for us. Jesus can help with his amazing power. Give everyone paper and instructions to make an origami boat (again, the internet will supply the necessary instructions – young children could be given cut out shapes of a boat to stick on a sheet of blue paper instead). Write the prayer on the boat and see if it floats in the bath or sink at home.

We all go through difficult times and it is good to have Jesus with us, just as he was with the disciples. His almighty power is able to keep our lives calm and on course. Show PowerPoint slides of boats and stormy seas whilst you invite everyone, or a group of volunteers, to make an origami boat following your instructions. Reflect on some personal storms that have happened in your life. What practical steps can be taken to remember to call on Jesus for help?

Lord, please help me to trust you more even when life gets rough. Amen.

How can we show that we love Jesus
By doing the things that Jesus says
How can we show our love for Father
By being his children who obey

What kind of man is Jesus?
What kind of man is he?
He can still the strongest wind
And make calm the roughest sea

How do we know that we love Jesus?
By doing the things that Jesus says.
How do we show our love for Father?
By being his children who obey.

Ian Smale

THE BEAUTY OF GOD

Revelation 21:18
The wall was made of jasper, and the city of pure gold, as pure as glass.

Black paper; thin card; acetates; acetate pens; cellophane sweet wrappers; scissors; craft knives; glue; double-sided tape.

For over one thousand years people have been making stained glass windows for churches. The coloured glass is often cut and shaped into pictures of well known Bible stories. There are two ways to make a stained glass effect bookmark – option 2 is more appropriate for young children.

Option 1:

- Using an acetate marker pen draw a window size 3.5cm wide by 13.5cm long onto a clear acetate sheet and mark in lots of pane shapes.
- Colour the window with marker pens on the opposite side to avoid the colour bleeding into the black lines.
- Cut out your stained glass effect (acetate) window leaving 0.5cm all the way round.
- Cut two pieces of card 4.75cm x 15cm to make the book mark.
- Using the exact width and height of your stained glass window, mark out where you want the window to fit.
- Using a sharp craft knife (supervise children) cut both pieces of card at the same time. (It helps to stick together with a little double sided tape to keep it in place.)
- Put double sided tape around the entire window opening and all of the edges on one piece of card.
- Carefully place the acetate window over the opening.
- Carefully place the second card on top.
- Finish as desired: you could write a prayer, add a tassel or trim off the corners.

Option 2:

- Pleat a piece of black paper concertina-style and cut out small shapes along the folds.
- Unfold and glue the cellophane sweet wrappers on the back so they cover the holes.

Fix the bookmarks temporarily to a window. The light shining through coloured glass reminds us of God's glory.

If you have stained glass windows in your church, explain their stories. As light streams through stained glass windows we are reminded of God's beauty, and the story of God's people. Allow people time to reflect on the beauty of the windows and the light pouring through them as you pray.

Dear God, you are so beautiful.
We are filled with wonder at the colour and light that streams from you into everything you have made. Amen.

Song:
The earth is filled with glorious things
Glorious things
Made by God above
The earth is filled with glorious things
But the greatest thing of all is God's love.

The seas are filled with glorious things
Glorious things
Made by God above
The seas are filled with glorious things
But the greatest thing of all is God's love.

The heavens are filled with glorious things
Glorious things
Made by God above
The heavens are filled with glorious things
But the greatest thing of all is God's love.

Everywhere around me I see glorious things
Glorious things
Made by God above
Everywhere around me I see glorious things
But the greatest thing of all is God's love.

Ian Smale

THE CROSS

Romans 5:8

But God demonstrates his own love for us in this: While we were still sinners, Christ died for us.

A4 card; scissors; sticky tape; post-it notes; pens.

Make a large cross by joining three pieces of white card lengthwise. Add two pieces of card crosswise as in the diagram below. Fix the cross to a wall. Invite people to think of something to ask or tell God and write, or draw a simple picture of their prayer on a post-it note. In turn, stick prayers to the cross, trusting God to answer them in the way he knows best.

Make a cross from white card and fix it to a wall or, if you have a large wooden cross, you could use that instead. After brief, grateful reflection on our ability to trust God to do what is best, give everyone opportunity to thank, ask or tell him heartfelt thoughts and requests. These can be drawn or written on post-it notes and brought to stick on the cross with full and joyful confidence that God will do what's right for us.

Dear Lord Jesus, thank you for dying for me on the cross. Amen.

But God demonstrates his own love for us,
His own love for us, yeah, own love for us
Because while we were still sinners
Christ died for us.

Ian Smale

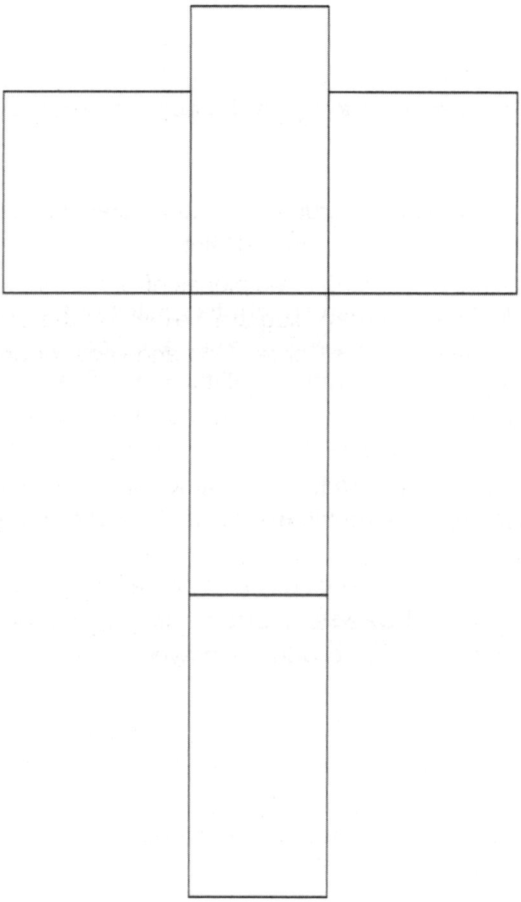

THE HEAVENS

Psalm 103:11
For as high as the heavens are above the earth, so great is his love for those who fear him.

Thin card; paper; paints & brushes, pastels, crayons, cans of spray paint, felt pens (as appropriate); scissors; PowerPoint display.

Draw onto thin card and then cut out templates of the sun, the moon and a star. Talk briefly about the differences in the sky at different times of day and night and how God created the sun, moon and all the stars. Draw pictures of a daytime or night-time sky using paints, pastels, crayons, or spray paints. The templates can be laid on the picture and coloured over with crayons or spray paints to reveal the sun, moon or stars. Alternatively draw round the outlines on separate sheets of paper, cut out and stick on the picture. Write the Bible verse on the picture.

Ask people to think of the best day or night sky they have seen, perhaps on holiday or at home. Show a PowerPoint display of skyscapes (include sunrise, day time, sunset and night time), some with the prayer written over the pictures.

Dear Lord, you created the heavens and the earth.
Please inspire me to be more creative when I praise and worship you. Amen.

For as high as the heavens are above the earth
For as high as the heavens are above the earth
So great is his love
So great is his love
So great is his love for those who fear him.

Ian Smale

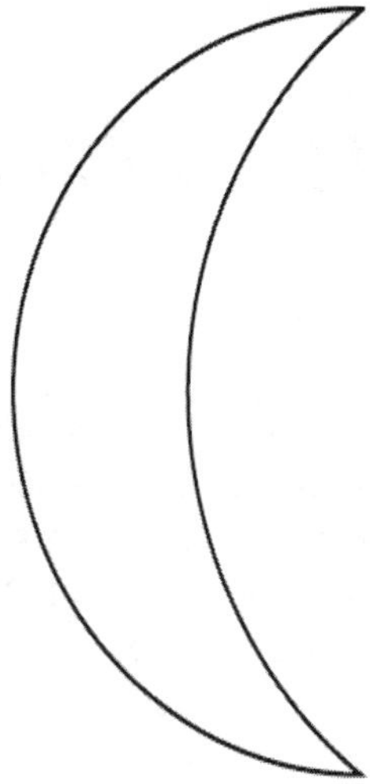

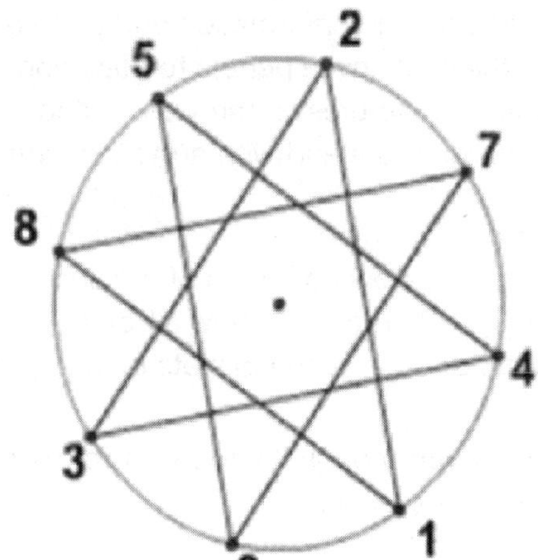
2
5
7
8
4
3
1
6

2
5
4
3
1

THE UNIVERSE

Hebrews 11:1–3

Now faith is being sure of what we hope for and certain of what we do not see. This is what the ancients were commended for. By faith we understand that the universe was formed at God's command, so that what is seen was not made out of what was visible.

An illustrated encyclopaedia, or appropriate information and pictures printed from a web site (start by checking out a site like *Wikipedia*); paper; crayons; felt pens; an orrery (if you are able to borrow one) or PowerPoint display.

We live in the Milky Way galaxy in a vast universe made by God. We can only see a very small part of our galaxy with its planets, moons and stars, but we know that the rest is out there in the far, far distance. Show the information and pictures of planets. Can you name the planets around the sun? Invite people to copy some of the close-up pictures of the planets and fix the pictures to the wall or floor in their order of distance from the sun. Invite everyone to stand with arms stretched out, fingertip to fingertip and say the prayer.

See if you can find someone with an orrery (a working model of the sun and the planets) and ask the owner to set it up for you. Alternatively show a PowerPoint display of our solar system. Ask everyone to try and name the planets in order.

Thank you God for making the universe. Even though it's too vast for us to see it all we can see your power at work in our lives. Amen.

Now faith is being sure of what we hope for
And certain of what we do not see
Faith is being sure of what we hope for
And certain of what we do not see.
I need faith, I need faith Lord, I need more faith
I need to be sure of what I can't see.
I need faith I need faith.
O Lord please help me
Lord, please give more faith to me.

Ian Smale

HEAR

BELLS

Exodus 28:35

The sound of the bells will be heard when he (Aaron) enters the Holy Place before the Lord and when he comes out.

A selection of bells in different sizes and sounds.

In Bible times different bells were used in worship and prayer. Long ago, before most people had clocks, church bells were rung when it was time for worship. They were sometimes rung as a warning in time of trouble, or for joy on special occasions. Ask if people have heard church bells – where and when? Slowly read Psalm 100. Each person can take it in turn to ring a bell for each line. Then ring all the bells together and ask everyone to repeat the prayer after you.

In Bible times bells signified holiness, prayer and worship. The priest had bells sewn into the hem of his robe to ring while he was in the Holy Place. A rope was tied to his ankle; if the bells stopped ringing, it was presumed he had died in God's holy presence. The people were not allowed to enter the sanctuary, so they tugged the rope to check whether they should pull the priest out. Invite reflection on God's holiness and our access into his presence. Ask people to come and pray, ringing a bell of their choice.

Dear Lord,
please help me to remember when I pray that I enter into your Holy presence. Amen.

Praise and glory
To the name of Jesus
Holy is his name

Praise and glory
To the name of Jesus
Holy is his name

Ian Smale

CLAPPING

Revelation 9:9

The sound of their wings was like the thundering of many horses and chariots rushing into battle.

Clapping instruments: castanets, rhythm sticks, coconut halves, blocks, etc.

Experiment with the instruments. In Bible times people used instruments similar to these to thank, praise and worship God. Ask everyone to think of something to thank God for, and choose an instrument. In turn, they can whisper their thanks, clap once, repeat their thanks and clap twice. When everyone has had a turn, repeat thanks all together continually, building up the volume in voice and clapping until very loud. Give the signal to stop.

In Bible times wooden sticks called clappers or wooden cymbals called *kymbe* (hollow cup-shaped bowls) were clapped together in ceremonial worship. Invite the Holy Spirit to inspire God's people today in holy, joyous worship in both old and new ways. Encourage everyone to begin clapping gently, whispering names and words for God. Increase the vocal and clapping volume to thundering then signal stop and begin again. Everyone can clap quietly while the prayer is slowly read.

Wonderful God, accept our praise and thanks today.
We bless your holy name. Amen.

Let's form a band together
Let's form a band together
Let's form a band together
And worship him whom we adore
Let's form a band together
Let's form a band together
Let's form a band together
And praise the risen Lord

Let's all praise together

Lets all clap together

Let's raise our hands together

Let's all dance together

It's great to be together

Ian Smale

CYMBALS

2 Samuel 6:5

David and the whole house of Israel were celebrating with all their might before the Lord, with songs and with harps, lyres, tambourines, sistrums and cymbals.

Materials to make simple instruments e.g. clean, empty yoghurt pots; tall crisp-containers; 15cm wide dowelling in various lengths; sandpaper; coloured paper; glue; rice; macaroni; saucepan lids; forked twigs or branches; elastic; tambourines; shakers, etc.

In advance, make one or two instruments for everyone to see and help them create their own. The sistrum was a triangular-shaped metal rattle. To make one, use a forked twig or small branch, thread macaroni onto thin elastic and zig-zag tie the elastic across the twig. Talk about different ways to praise God and worship him. Learn the song without instruments. Pray the prayer together, holding up instruments and make a worship march, singing and using instruments with all your might.

In Bible times various percussion instruments were used to praise God. Cymbals of different kinds filled the temple with whirring, quivering and clashing. Hand out instruments (or use those that have been made in the activity time). Use them to praise God freely.

Lord, please help me to praise you with all of my might. Amen.

In the front are the singers
After them the musicians
And then come the girls
With the tambourines

Praise God in this great congregation
Praise God in this great congregation
Praise God in this great congregation
Let this great congregation praise God.

Ian Smale

IDEA 24

EARS TO HEAR

Isaiah 50:4

The Sovereign Lord has given me an instructed tongue, to know the word that sustains the weary. He wakens me morning by morning, wakens my ear to listen like one being taught.

Items that make sounds: e.g. mobile phone (ringtone), alarm clock, vacuum cleaner; electric whisk, radio, etc.

Put the items behind a screen. Have a pre-selected volunteer whom everyone knows hidden behind the screen. Get the volunteer to activate sounds for the audience to guess. Then the volunteer says, 'When God speaks, we can hear him.' Who is it? When we know someone, we recognise their voice. When we get to know God, we know his voice, too. Pray the prayer together, touching ears, head and heart.

Play the same game as above. When we know someone, we recognise their voice. When we get to know God, we know his voice, too. Reflect on the fact that only humans are created to hear God. How does God speak? Pray the prayer together, touching ears, head and heart.

Father God, please help me to listen to you in whatever way you choose to speak to me and to do what you tell me. Amen.

The Lord wakes me every morning.
He even wakes my ear.
The Lord wakes me every morning,
For there's things I need to hear.
Lord tell me what you want to say.
I need to hear it and obey.
'Cause it's the start of a brand new day
To be with my friend Jesus.

Ian Smale

GOD SPEAKING

1 Samuel 3:10–11

The Lord came and stood there, calling as at other times, "Samuel! Samuel!" Then Samuel said, "Speak, for your servant is listening." And the Lord said to Samuel, "See, I am about to do something in Israel that will make the ears of everyone who hears of it tingle."

In advance write on four small pieces of card: With a voice. In a dream. A message for us given to someone else. In our minds.

Wobble your fingers on your throat, saying 'Aaaah'. The vocal cords in our throats are like folds of stretched skin. When we breathe in the air goes over them, and they vibrate and make sound. That's how we speak and sing. How does God speak to us? Play a hunting game. Send a volunteer out while you hide one of the cards. When they come back have everyone hum louder or softer as the seeker gets nearer or further away until the card is found. Read the card and repeat the game with the other three.

Preselect a volunteer to mime the sentence, 'Speak for your servant is listening.'

Ask everyone to guess the sentence. Invite people to share about how God has spoken to them in the past.

Lord, please help me to listen and hear what you want to say to me. Amen.

Let God speak and I will listen
Let God speak there's things I'm needing to put right
Let God speak and I will obey what he says
Please God, I want to hear your voice tonight.
Lord I want to hear your voice tonight.

Ian Smale

GOD'S PEACE

John 14:27

Peace I leave with you; my peace I give you. I do not give to you as the world gives. Do not let your hearts be troubled and do not be afraid.

Mobile phone and charger; felt pens; acrylic pastels or crayons; paper; PowerPoint display.

If possible go outside or open doors and windows. What can we hear? We enjoy being with others, busy and noisy. Show the mobile phone, preferably with it showing the battery is low. I've used my phone lots of times and now it needs recharging. Sleep recharges us, but sometimes we need God to give us an extra charge of his peace. Invite people to share their idea of a peaceful place and sound. Try to imagine the places and recreate the sounds together. Offer paper, pens and pastels and invite people to quietly draw the things that worry and concern them. On the other side of the paper they can draw things that bring peace to mind and heart, and make a resolve to seek them out often.

Show a PowerPoint display of visuals that represent peace (if you have done the activity above try and include pictures of places that were mentioned) and overlay the Bible verse on some of them. Encourage everyone to meditate on the things that cause God's peace to be disrupted. Then, with a background of peaceful music, consider the things that bring peace to mind and heart, and make a resolve to seek them out often.

Thank you Lord that in a world that always seems to be full of noise and worry you give us peace. Amen.

Song:

You give me peace in a world
Where confusion seems to have control
And joy when depression
Surrounds me from all sides.
You give me love in my heart
When hatred tries to pull me down.
But the best thing that you gave me is my life,
And I'd never be able to thank you enough
If I spent forever trying to
I'd never be able to praise you
In the way that it should be
So I offer you in worship
The only thing I have to give you
O Lord here I am please accept me.

Ian Smale

IDEA 27

GOD'S VOICE

1 Kings 19:12

After the earthquake came a fire, but the Lord was not in the fire. And after the fire came a gentle whisper.

2m bright red fabric (Chinese silk or similar).

Form two teams facing each other. Give one word of a sentence to each team member. (If there are more than seven in a team, two or more can have the same word. If there are less than seven in a team, two words can be allocated to some people). After 1–2–3 the first team all shout their given words loudly at the same time. The other team has to try to guess the sentence. Swap over. Sometimes we need a quiet space to hear God.

Sentences: Team 1 – Why can't I hear what God says? Team 2 – God doesn't seem to talk to me.

Ask for seven (or fourteen) volunteers. Play the game above with everyone trying to guess the two sentences. Then, have two people each take an end of the red fabric. They can wave it up and down in big, slow arm movements as in a wind storm. Then shake the fabric quickly like a shuddering earthquake. Next, they can turn it sideways to make the fire. Finally they can put it on the floor quietly. Display the prayer and pray it together.

Lord thank you that you want to speak to us. Help me sometimes to be still so I can hear your voice more clearly.

A powerful wind tore the mountains apart,
Apart, apart,
But the Lord was not in the wind.
After the wind there was an earthquake,
An earthquake, an earthquake,
But the Lord was not in the earthquake.
After the earthquake came a fire,
A fire, a fire,
But the Lord was not in the fire.
After the fire came a still small voice
A voice, a voice
And that was the voice of God.

Ian Smale

LOUD VOICES

Revelation 7:10

And they cried out in a loud voice: "Salvation belongs to our God, who sits on the throne, and to the Lamb."

Picture of the Lamb of God; pens.

In Bible times, when people knew they deserved to be punished for their sin, they would sometimes kill an animal in their place, asking God to forgive them. In the Bible, Jesus is called the Lamb of God because he was killed in our place, for the wrong we do. Give everyone a picture of the Lamb of God. Younger children can colour the picture and copy the words: Thank you Jesus for taking away the sins of the world. Others can write their own thanks to Jesus for his sacrifice on their behalf around and over the picture. Join together to say the prayer.

In the book of Revelation Jesus is called the Lamb of God. *Agnus Dei* is the Latin phrase for Lamb of God, and the *Agnus Dei* prayer in Latin and English is offered in many church services as part of the Communion. Invite people to speak out prayers thanking Jesus for his sacrifice on their behalf; then, all together, have everyone say the *Agnus Dei* prayer (in either Latin, English or both).

Agnus Dei, qui tollis peccata mundi, miserere nobis.
Agnus Dei, qui tollis peccata mundi, miserere nobis.
Agnus Dei, qui tollis peccata mundi, dona nobis pacem.

Lamb of God, who take away the sins of the world, have mercy upon us.
Lamb of God, who take away the sins of the world, have mercy upon us.
Lamb of God, who take away the sins of the world, grant us peace.

And the people cried
With their voices loud,
Salvation belongs to our God
Who sits on the throne
And to the Lamb
Who sits on the throne
And to the Lamb.

Ian Smale

MAKING MUSIC

1 Corinthians 14:7–8

Even in the case of lifeless things that make sounds, such as the flute or harp, how will anyone know what tune is being played, unless there is a distinction in the notes? Again if the trumpet does not sound a clear call, who will get ready for battle?

Musicians and instruments; screen. (Encourage everyone who plays instruments to bring them along.)

In advance, hide some musicians behind a screen or just outside your meeting room. In turn they can briefly play some music and people can guess the instrument. Give an opportunity for anyone else to play their own instruments whilst others clap or tap in rhythm. God wants us to make music for him. It makes him glad and as we play, it makes us happy too. Tap the rhythm of the prayer line by line as you say it.

Have your organist, band, or a pianist play extracts from several familiar hymns or songs with such flowery accompaniment that it's impossible to hear their melody line, or even recognise it. Have them gradually de-construct the music until someone can guess correctly. It's hard to enjoy music that is meaningless. God enjoys worship that is full of meaning, and so do his people.

Heavenly Father, thank you for creating musical instruments that give us joy, especially when we play them for you. Amen.

Let everyone who worships God be happy and be glad
Let everyone who worships God be happy and be glad
Let everyone who worships God be happy and be glad

Let everyone who worships God play the noisy drums

Let everyone who worships God play the lead guitar

Let everyone who worships God play the piano

And be happy and be glad.

Ian Smale

MOUTH

Psalm 141:3–4

Set a guard over my mouth, O Lord; keep watch over the door of my lips. Let not my heart be drawn to what is evil.

Clean old socks; scissors; red, brown and blue felt; glue.

Show everyone how to make sock puppets:

- Using the felt, cut out red tongues and brown or blue eyes.
- Pull the sock right over one hand.
- Push in the mouth and glue a tongue inside.
- Stick eyes in position.

Ask questions that volunteers can answer using their puppet.

Sometimes we say hurtful or bad things with our mouths. God wants us to think before we open our mouths to speak. Use the puppets as you pray aloud.

Display the Bible verse on a screen. Invite a few volunteers to come to the front and make sock puppets or use your puppet team if you have one. Everyone should say the Bible verse together and then the prayer. Everyone can mouth the prayer back, either using puppets or by making a mouth with their hand.

Dear Lord, please help me only to say things that are good and helpful. Amen.

Set a guard over my mouth, O Lord,
Keep watch over the door of my lips,
Let not my heart be drawn to what is evil.

Ian Smale

QUIET WORDS

Ecclesiastes 9:17
The quiet words of the wise are more to be heeded than the shouts of a ruler of fools.

Paper; pens; a flipchart; Bibles.

Jesus told stories, often called parables, which carried an important message. Put people in mixed-age groups of three or four. There are lots of parables in the Gospels (see the list below). Challenge the groups to list as many as they can. (You could give out Bibles to help if you wish.) The winning team can choose a parable to act out simply. A few props can be improvised. Ask everyone else to decide on the message of the parable. Jesus said people who are ready to hear his important message will hear his quiet words. Invite people to place their hands on the Bibles and pray.

A parable is a story with a hidden meaning. Jesus told lots of parables to help people understand more about God. He said that those who are ready to hear will find his hidden meaning, his quiet words. Invite people to call out parables and write them on the flipchart (see list below). Have your drama group prepared to act out a parable of your choice or ask for volunteers to simply act out one as you read it from the Bible. Hold up Bibles and pray.

Lord, thank you for all the wonderful stories we can enjoy in the Bible.
Please help us to hear your quiet words. Amen.

As I sit quietly
Ever so quietly
Arms by my side
Ears open wide
Help me to listen

As people now teach me
More of the stories of Jesus

Ian Smale

<u>Parables in the Gospels</u>

Fishing net (Matthew 13:47–50)
Forgiven debts (Luke 7:41–43)
Friend at midnight (Luke 11:5–8)
Good Samaritan (Luke 10:30–37)
Great feast (Luke 14:16–24)
Growing wheat (Mark 4:26–29)
Loaned money (Matthew 25:14–30)
Lost coin (Luke 15:8–10)
Lost sheep (Matthew 18:12–14; Luke 15:3–7)
Lost son (Luke 15:11–32)
Marriage feast (Matthew 22:1–14)
Mustard seed (Matthew 13:31–32; Mark 4:30–32; Luke 13:18–19)
Nobleman's servants (Luke 19:11–27)
Pearl (Matthew 13:45–46)
Proud Pharisee and the corrupt tax collector (Luke 18:9–14)
Rich fool (Luke 12:16–21)
Servant's role (Luke 17:7–10)
Shrewd manager (Luke 16:1–9)
Sower and the soil (Matthew 13:3–8; Mark 4:3–8; Luke 8:5–8; 11–15)
Ten virgins (Matthew 25:1–13)
Travelling owner of the house (Mark 13:34–37)
Treasure (Matthew 13:44)
Two sons (Matthew 21:28–32)
Unforgiving servant (Matthew 18:23–35)
Unjust judge (Luke 18:1–8)
Unproductive fig tree (Luke 13:6–9)
Wedding feast (Luke 14:7–11)
Weeds (Matthew 13:24–30)
Wicked tenants (Matthew 21:33–34; Mark 12:1–9; Luke 20:9–16)
Wise and faithful servants (Matthew 24:45–51; Luke 12:42–48)
Workers in the harvest (Matthew 20:1–16)
Yeast (Matthew 13:38; Luke 13:20–21)

RAIN

Isaiah 55:10–11

As the rain and snow come down from heaven, and do not return to it without watering the earth and making it bud and flourish, so that it yields seed for the sower and bread for the eater, so is my word that goes out from my mouth: It will not return to me empty, but will accomplish what I desire and achieve the purpose for which I sent it.

As many rain stick shakers as you can borrow; long cardboard tubes; dress-makers pins; rice or lentils; tape; paper; pen; basket.

Identify different kinds of weather: wind, sun, snow, hailstones, rain, fog or mist, ice and frost. Some may seem to have no identifiable sound, but if they did have one, what might it be? Work out sounds and actions for each of them. Make rain stick shakers:

- Draw a criss-cross spiral formation on the tube as below.
- Push the dressmaking pins through the tube at regular spaces going down the tube.
- Tape up the bottom end of the tube securely.
- Put the lentils or rice into the tube.
- Tape up the top end of the tube securely.
- You can finish off your rain stick by covering it in adhesive or brown paper to cover up the pins and paint a pattern on it

Use the rain stick shakers or drumming fingers for rain. Use actions in the song.

Write out weather sounds and place in the basket (e.g. rain on a tent; silent snow; wind in the trees; popping seeds in hot sun; hailstones on the car; muffled ships horn in the fog; cracking ice on the lake.) Choose an 'orchestra' to play the rain stick shakers and pass the basket around. Signal the orchestra to stop at intervals and the person holding the basket can read out the phrase and thank God for that kind of weather.

Lord, please help me to praise you for the rain and the sun, and EVERY kind of weather. Amen.

When God sends rain
I put my boots and coat on,
just as I am told.
When God sends snow
I put my gloves and hat on
So I won't get cold.
But when God's sun comes shining through
That's the weather I like best
Off come my boots
Off comes my coat
Off come my gloves
Off comes my hat
On goes my swimming costume
As I don't need all the rest.

Ian Smale

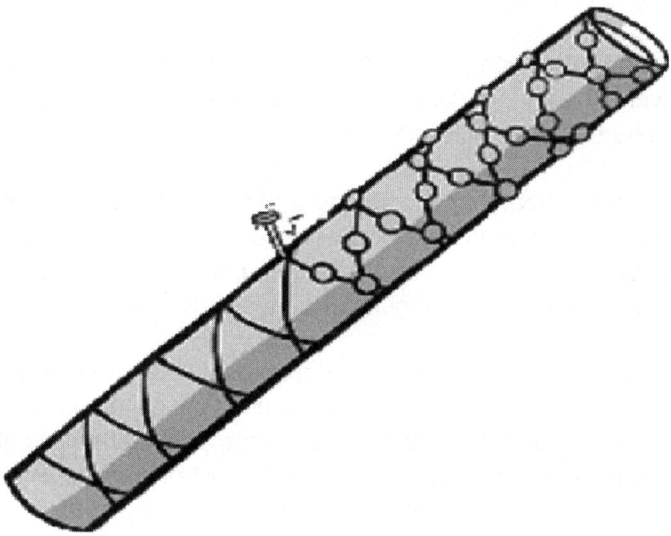

IDEA 33

RHYTHM

1 John 5:4–5

For everyone born of God overcomes the world. This is the victory that has overcome the world, even our faith. Who is it that overcomes the world? Only he who believes that Jesus is the Son of God.

Large coffee tins with plastic lids (alternatively use carpet tubes or plastic flower pots with a heavy-duty plastic top held in place with strong elastic bands); stickers or coloured paper, scissors and glue to decorate.

'Rhythm has a beat and a time and a movement.' Tap your fingers on the table in rhythm with the sentence. Repeat several times, inviting everyone to join in. Make and decorate simple drums together. Listen to the song and then sing with drum accompaniment. Try singing, drumming and marching at the same time.

Timbrels and tabrets were drum-like instruments used in Bible times that were struck rhythmically with the hand. Give out drums and tambourines to volunteers (use the ones you made in the activity time if appropriate) and have everyone else stand so they can beat on the back of the seat in front of them (or with one hand on their other). Beat in time as you sing the song below or establish a rhythm of one long beat followed by three short ones as you recite Psalm 18:31–35.

Lord, please help us not to give up when times get hard but to march on and keep going. Amen.

We are marching along to the rhythm of the drum
In God's army we have a lot of fun
Even when the battle's hard we know we'll overcome –
When Jesus died the war was won.

Ian Smale

ROARING LIONS

Proverbs 28:1

The wicked man flees though no-one pursues, but the righteous are as bold as a lion.

Whiteboard or flipchart; thin card; craft sticks or thin elastic; scissors; sticky tape; pens; yellow and orange crêpe paper, tissue paper and/or wool for decoration.

Why do you think the lion is called the king of all animals? Lions are strong and brave, and not afraid. One of the names for Jesus is 'Lion of Judah' because he's strong and brave and not afraid. Using the template below, everyone can make and decorate lion masks. See how loud you can roar as you sing the song.

Draw a simple lion's head on the whiteboard or flipchart from the template below. The lion was common in Old Testament times and is mentioned over one hundred and thirty times in the Bible. The lion was a symbol of royalty, and one of the names for Jesus is 'Lion of Judah' meaning he is brave and bold. Ask people to suggest situations when they need the bravery and boldness of Jesus, the Lion of Judah, and write them on the whiteboard/flipchart around the lion's head. As you write up each situation, pray the prayer and then invite everyone (especially the children) to roar loudly.

Dear Lord Jesus, please help me to be brave and bold like you. Amen.

The wicked run away though no one's chasing them
The wicked run away though no one's chasing them
The wicked run away though no one's chasing them
But the righteous are as bold as a lion.
Roar roar, Lion of Judah make us more like you
Roar roar, Lion of Judah.
No more fear
Just sincere
And righteous through and through.

Ian Smale

SINGING TO GOD

Psalm 68:4–6

Sing to God, sing praise to his name, extol him who rides upon the clouds – his name is the Lord – and rejoice before him.

There are many ways to praise God and singing is one of them. Some of us may be shy about using our voices to sing, or think that we don't sing very well. But the most important thing is that we sing our praises to God with love. In the Bible King David had singers and musicians in his choir, and we're going to sing one of his songs. I wonder if it sounded like this. Learn the harmonies and sing the song below confidently.

Have the musicians bring some songs that have simple harmonies for everyone to learn, dividing the congregation into different parts. Many people today don't learn to harmonise in singing yet it can add a greater dimension to praise. King David appointed men from the tribe of Levi to be singers and musicians in his choir. Try singing one of King David's songs (the song below).

Dear Lord Jesus, please help me to use my voice to sing and praise you more. Amen.

Let's sing to the Lord
Let's praise his holy name
Extol him who rides upon the cloud
His name is the Lord
Let all the earth rejoice
And children let's praise him
Children let's praise him
Children let's praise him
Children let's praise him out loud

For he's a father to the fatherless
Defender of the widow
He's God in his holy dwelling
He loves to put the lonely in a family
And the prisoner follows him singing
So children let's praise him
Children let's praise him
Children let's praise him out loud.

Ian Smale

IDEA 36

STRINGED INSTRUMENTS

1 Chronicles 15:16

David told the leaders of the Levites to appoint their brothers as singers to sing joyful songs, accompanied by musical instruments: lyres, harps and cymbals.

Flipchart; pens; tissue boxes, or other cardboard boxes with a hole cut in the front; elastic bands of varying thickness; materials for decoration.

Invite a musician to play a stringed instrument, or play a CD of instrumental string music, as you do this activity. In Bible times they used lots of stringed instruments, just as we do today. Invite everyone to make and decorate a zither or harp with boxes and elastic bands. Play them as you sing the song below, and pray together.

Draw a large, simple guitar shape on the flipchart. Find as many strings instrumentalists as you can and invite them to give a brief demonstration. In the Old Testament musical instruments were used to express praise to God. In Genesis 4:21 we read about Jubal, the first person in the Bible to invent musical instruments like the harp and the flute. The harp was sometimes called a *kinnor* (usually made of cypress wood and the only stringed instrument to be mentioned in the first five books of the Bible). The Aramaic word for harp is *qitros* and is where we get the word 'guitar' from. The *psaltery* was a smaller type of harp plucked by the fingers and it was also called a *nebel*, viol or lute and could have up to ten strings. David was able to play both the *kinnor* and *nebel* which made a bass sound. The *sambyke* was a triangular shaped harp with four or more strings and made a high pitched sound. Invite people to tell of a time when music played an important part in their lives and write it on the guitar on the flipchart.

Thank you Lord for the gift of music. Amen.

Let's thank the Lord for music and the sounds that can be made
Let's join in with the piano as we hear it played.

Let's thank the Lord for music and the sounds that can be made
Let's join in with the piccolo as we hear it played.

Let's thank the Lord for music and the sounds that can be made
Let's join in with the violin as we hear it played.

Let's thank the Lord for music and the sounds that can be made
Let's join in with the mandolin as we hear it played.

Ian Smale

THUNDER

Job 37:3–4

He unleashes his lightning beneath the whole heaven and sends it to the ends of the earth. After that comes the sound of his roar; he thunders with his majestic voice. When his voice resounds, he holds nothing back.

A variety of things to create the sound of thunder: metal trays, gravel, wobble boards, drums, saucepan lids, etc.; paper; pens.

Invite everyone to experiment by sliding gravel around metal trays, or using the other objects plus their hands and feet, to make sound effects for thunder. Put all the sounds together to make a huge thunder crash. In turn, ask everyone to name something they are afraid of, followed by their thunder sound effect. Pray the prayer below together.

Draw a simple thunder cloud, photocopy and give a copy to everyone as they come in. Invite people to write or draw on their cloud some things they are afraid of. Have someone read Psalm 46, dramatically and with plenty of expression and then invite everyone to make their response to God, writing or drawing over their fears.

Lord, we thank you that you are so powerful.

We need never be afraid of thunder and loud noises because you promise to take care of us. Amen.

I once was frightened of spiders
I once was frightened of the dark
I once was frightened by many, many things
Especially things that barked
But now I'm asking Jesus to help those fears to go
'Cause I don't want them to be part of me no no no no no

I once was frightened of thunder
And frightened of lightning too
I once was frightened by many, many things
That crashed and banged and blew
But now I'm asking Jesus to help those fears to go
'Cause I don't want them to be part of me no no no no no

Ian Smale

TRUMPET

1 Thessalonians 4:16

For the Lord himself will come down from heaven, with a loud command, with the voice of the archangel, and with the trumpet call of God, and the dead in Christ will rise first.

Plastic bottles; plastic tubing that fits the neck of the bottles; paper; scissors; felt pens; sticky tape.

If you know a trumpeter, invite them to come and play. Alternatively use a CD of trumpet music (*And the trumpet shall sound* from *Young Messiah* CD would be particularly appropriate). In Bible times there were many trumpet instruments. It takes a lot of practice to learn to play a trumpet. Make 'trumpets'.

Option 1:

- Cut the base off a plastic bottle.
- Insert a length of tubing into the neck of the bottle that is long enough to hold and tape in place.
- Decorate the bottle.
- Blow as hard as you can to make a trumpet sound.

Option 2 (young children may find it too hard to get a sound from the instrument above):

- Decorate and pattern one side of a large sheet of paper.
- Roll the paper into a cone shape and fix in place with sticky tape.
- Toot to make a trumpet sound.

Use the instruments to replace the hallelujahs in the chorus of the song.

In Bible times there were lots of trumpet-like instruments. The pipe or *halil* was used in festival or funeral processions and it was a plaintive sound made by blowing through reeds. The player usually carried spare reeds around with him in a little box or bag. The flute or *masroqita* made a whistling or hissing sound. The organ or *ugab* was the name for a collection of pipe instruments. The horn or *qeren* was used either for carrying oil or as a small trumpet. The *shofar* was a long horn with a turned up end and was the national trumpet of the Israelites and is still used in Jewish synagogues today. Trumpets can be played for all kinds of occasions from celebration to the evocative. The Bible tells us that when Jesus returns in clouds of glory from heaven, there will be an amazing trumpet call of God. If you have a trumpeter or other brass instrumentalists among your musicians, ask them to play a fanfare before the prayer; alternatively use CD.

Lord, may my life be a joyful noise to you as I wait for your trumpet call. Amen.

We'll praise him on the trumpet and we'll praise him on guitar
We'll praise him with a drum and with a harp and with a lyre
We'll praise him with our voices 'cause we want to lift him higher
And all God's people shout hallelujah!

Hallelujah, hallelujah, hallelujah, hallelujah, hallelujah, hallelujah
And all God's people shout hallelujah!

We'll praise him for his favour and we'll praise him for his deeds,
We'll praise him though the road is rough he's still the one who leads,
We'll praise him for provision as he cares for all our needs.

We'll praise him that upon a cross the Lamb of God was slain,
We'll praise him that he conquered death and now he lives again,
We'll praise him He's the King of kings who will forever reign.

We'll praise him that He's making us the people we should be
We'll praise him that our chains are gone, we're now completely free,
We'll praise him we don't know defeat, we live in victory
And all God's people shout hallelujah!

Ian Smale

WHISPERING POWER

Psalm 107:29
He stilled the storm to a whisper; the waves of the sea were hushed.

A play parachute or a length of blue/turquoise fabric (Chinese silk or similar).

Tell the story of Jesus calming the storm (Mark 4:36–41). Invite people to share how they might have felt. Have volunteers firmly hold the parachute or fabric up high and ripple it in huge waves. Everyone else can run back and forth under it. Call out, 'Quiet! Be still!' and everyone must stand still and silent as the waves drop back to a gentle ripple. God's power is amazing! Pray and sing together.

There are several stories in the New Testament about Jesus calming storms, listed below. Play Chinese Whispers using some of the phrases from these verses e.g. Jesus said: Where is your faith?

Matthew 8:23–27
Luke 8:22–25
Mark 6:47–52
Mark 4:36–41
John 6:16–21

Lord, help me to know I am always safe with you by my side. Amen.

Jesus stilled the storm to a whisper
And the waves of the sea were hushed.

Jesus stilled the storm to a whisper
And the waves of the sea were hushed.

Noisy days rushing around
Quiet nights
I'm sleeping safe and sound.

Jesus stilled the storm to a whisper
And the waves of the sea were hushed.

Ian Smale

IDEA 40

WHISTLING WIND

Psalm 57:1

Have mercy on me, O God, have mercy on me, for in you my soul takes refuge. I will take refuge in the shadow of your wings until the disaster has passed.

Balloons; feathers.

Can you whistle? Allow time for demonstrations! Balloons can whistle. Blow up a balloon, stretch the necks sideways, and allow the air to escape making a whistling noise. Let volunteers (or everyone) take it in turn. Sometimes the wind whistles through a bird's feathers. Let everyone try to keep a feather in the air by whistling (younger children can just blow if they are unable to whistle). God says he will take care of us in the shadow of his wings. Identify people who need to be safe in the shadow of God's wings and pray for them.

Think of an eagle in a high mountain area, ready to fledge her young. Twig by twig she destroys the nest from under them until, totally exposed to the elements, they have no choice but to fly. She swoops through the air with the wind whistling over her outstretched feathers, underneath her chicks. God says he will keep us safe in the shadow of his wings. Invite people to name someone who needs that place of safety. Volunteers can choose a feather and whistle to keep it in the air while everyone else prays out for each of the identified people.

Dear Lord, I lift up (name) to you, they need your help right now.
Please take care of (name). Amen.

Be merciful to me O Lord
Be merciful,
Because I come to you for safety.
In the shadow of your wings

I find protection
Until the raging storms are over

Ian Smale

TOUCH

IDEA 41

A CROSS OF WOOD

Mark 6:3

Isn't this the carpenter? Isn't this Mary's son and the brother of James, Joseph, Judas and Simon?

Driftwood from the beach or bark or supple branches, like willow from woodland debris; string; strips of leather; scissors.

Display the assortment of wood and talk about things that are made from it. The cross upon which Jesus died was made from wood. Isn't it strange that the very material Jesus used in his everyday work was the instrument of his death? Jesus died so that we could be made right with God. Help everyone choose and shape some wood into a cross shape. Tie pieces together with string or strips of leather. Hold the crosses up while you pray.

In advance, make a cross as above. Pass the cross around for everyone to touch and feel as you allow time for meditation on the last hours of Jesus' life. He willingly allowed himself to be taken prisoner, was tortured, tried and killed so that we can find freedom.

Dear Lord Jesus, thank you for the cross and all the suffering you went through so I could be set free from all the bad things that tie me up. Amen.

No wooden cross could kill the Lord
Nor could the Roman's whip or spear
Neither Pilate, nor Judas, nor the devil himself,
With His life could interfere.
He gave his body for mankind
He gave his blood for you and me,
And in him sin was defeated,
In him we've victory.

Ian Smale

A CROSS REMINDER

Mark 8:34

If anyone would come after me, he must deny himself and take up his cross and follow me.

Air-hardening clay; flipchart; pens.

Jesus wants us to follow his ways, doing what's right and good. But sometimes we may not feel like it, or friends want us to do things that mean we would not be following Jesus. Invite everyone to use air-hardening clay to make a small cross shape. When it's tough to follow Jesus and to do what's right, hold your clay cross and ask Jesus to help you keep following him. Following Jesus is the best way and makes us glad.

Invite everyone to suggest times and places when following Jesus is hardest and then hand out small lumps of air-hardening clay so that everyone can make a small cross. Pray the prayer and encourage everyone to decide on a place to keep the cross as a future aid to prayer.

Dear Lord, each time I hold this cross please help me to remember what you have done for me and to follow you. Amen.

If I want to be a follower of Jesus
If I want to be a follower of Jesus
I must start life anew
And do things that he wants me to
And take up a cross which is hard to do
If I want to follow Jesus

Ian Smale

BINDING WORDS

Deuteronomy 6:8
Tie them as symbols on your hands and bind them on your foreheads.

Brightly coloured wool in different colours; small wooden beads; scissors; smooth string or cord.

Option 1: Make a prayer rope.

- Everyone will need 4m of smooth string or cord.
- Find the middle of the cord and make the first knot.
- Wind the cord around your index finger, winding backwards to form an X.
- Repeat twice more, forming three loops around the finger.
- Ease the three loops off your finger leaving a gap at the top above your nail.
- Thread the end of the cord through the gap out towards the end of your fingers. Try to leave the loops intact and in a straight row.
- Holding the cord with two fingers pull apart, slowly tightening and rolling the cord as you go. The loops should nest together in a row forming a long bead shape.
- Continue to make 7 groups of 3 knots 2cm apart.
- Join the loose ends together with the same type of knot, with two winds this time, and form a cross as on the template below.

Option 2 (for younger children): Make a Trinity bracelet.

- Cut three different coloured strands of wool that will break if it is caught and pulled tight, each about 50cm.
- Thread one wooden bead on each strand.
- Tie the strings together loosely, so they pass over the head with the beads lying together as a pendant. The strings and the beads are reminders of God the Father, Jesus the Son and the Holy Spirit.

The Bible tells us that when we know what God says we will live well and know what to do. In Bible times people made special arm and head ties called phylacteries to carry scriptures on them and remember what God said. Help children pray the prayer together.

In Deuteronomy 6:8 people were encouraged to follow God's wisdom and instruction carefully, and to wear his words around their hands, heads and heart as a constant reminder. Invite everyone to make a simple string neck cord. Either make a plait long enough to reach the heart, with two strands of three different colours of wool, joining and trimming the ends, or use three different coloured strands and thread three wooden beads on one of them to lie in the centre, representing the Holy Trinity. Pray the prayer together.

Heavenly Father, please help me to hear what you say, do it happily, and stay close to you forever. Amen.

Lord help me to do the things you say
Bind them upon my heart
And help me Lord walk in your way
That we may never part
All the things that I have heard
About Jesus from the living word
Bind them upon
Bind them upon
Bind them upon my heart.

Ian Smale

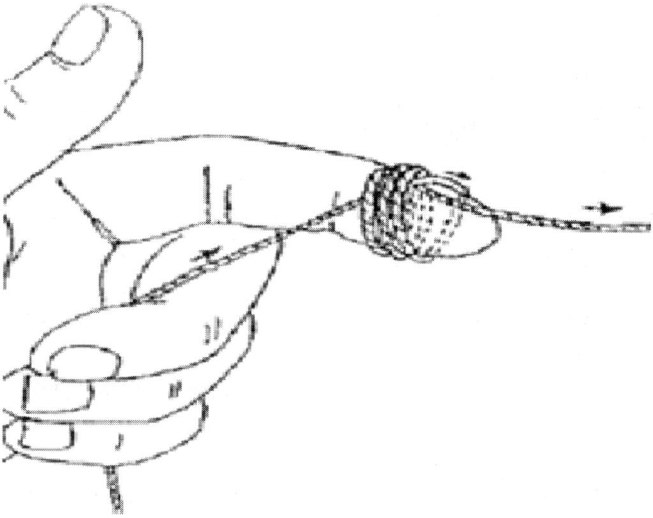

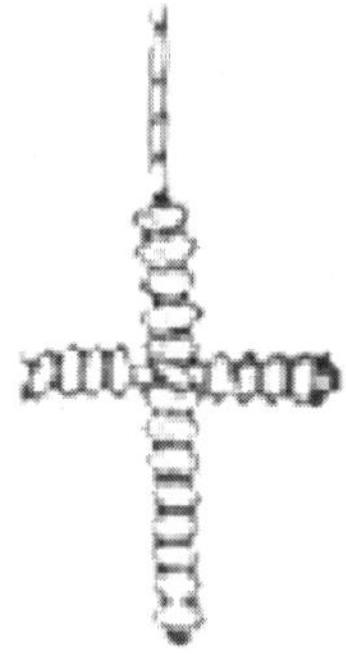

BROKEN CHAINS

Galatians 5:1
It is for freedom that Christ has set us free.

Strips of thin, coloured paper and glue sticks or bought paper chain paper; chain bought from a DIY store or ironmongers; silver wire; pliers.

Option 1: fashion crosses from silver wire and attach them to a length of chain.
Option 2: make lengths of paper chain and see who can make the longest paper chain. Now join them all together. Make a circle, holding the chain. Long ago, people in prison had chains put on their hands and feet. They had no hope of escape. The Bible tells us that when we do wrong things it's as if we are in chains, even though we can't see them. But when we believe that Jesus died to save us from our sins, he breaks those chains and we are free to love him and do what's right. Take home either the chains with a cross or a few links of the broken paper chain as a reminder that Jesus sets us free.

Give everyone the materials to make three or four paper chain links and join them all together. Ask people to briefly contemplate what their lives were like before they knew Christ, reminding them of the hymn that Charles Wesley wrote, 'My chains fell off, my heart was free, I rose, went forth, and followed thee.' The paper chains can be broken as a symbol of freedom to live Christ's way, and held up as the prayer is prayed. Links can be taken home and taped into your Bible as a reminder that Jesus sets us free.

Lord Jesus, thank you that you set me free through your death on the cross. Amen.

Where the Spirit of the Lord is there is freedom x 3
There is freedom where the Spirit of the Lord is.

So if the Son sets you free
You will be free indeed x 3
It is for freedom that Christ has set us free.

Ian Smale

COMMUNION CUP

Matthew 26:27–28

Then he took the cup, gave thanks and offered it to them, saying, 'Drink from it, all of you. This is my blood of the covenant, which is poured out for many for the forgiveness of sins.'

Air-hardening clay.

The cup used at the Last Supper was probably an earthenware bowl, large enough for everyone to use. Give everyone enough air-hardening clay to design their own special cup as a reminder of what Jesus has done for us on the cross.

Share communion together.

Dear Lord Jesus

We come in thanksgiving for your sacrifice for us on the cross. Your forgiveness for the wrong things we have done was immensely costly and we are eternally grateful. Amen.

Thank you Lord Jesus for the bread and the wine,
The bread's like your body that was broken for mine
The wine's like your blood that was shed so that we
Will never forget Calvary

You died for the world, you died for me
Hung on a cross in agony
Yet after three days you came back from the dead
We celebrate this with the wine and the bread.

Ian Smale

ENGRAVING

Isaiah 49:16

See, I have engraved you on the palms of my hands.

Card; wax crayons; black poster paint; brushes; pencils; wooden skewers or cocktail sticks.

Make scratch art boards:

- Colour the entire card by crayoning over it using a variety of bold colours. None of the card should show through.
- Paint over the whole card with black poster paint. The paint should cover the entire crayoning but not be so thick that it will crack when it dries.
- Leave to dry.

You either need to prepare these in advance or have everyone make one at the end of one activity time for use next time.

God tells us that he has engraved our name on his hands. Not just written. Written names might fade away. Our names are deeply scratched, engraved with love, on God's hands. Everyone can draw a design on their board with a pencil and then scratch into the paint to reveal the colours underneath. Hold up etched pictures and pray together.

Read the prayer. Repeat it word by word, spelling each word if necessary, and ask everyone to write out the words using a finger onto the palm of the other hand.

Lord Jesus, thank you for your hand upon my life. Amen.

I'll kiss the hand of Jesus yes I will,
I'll kiss the hand of Jesus yes I will,
As I see the hole where the nail has been, I realise it was my sin
That marred those beautiful hands, that scarred those beautiful hands.

The hand that held the little ones, sitting on his knee
The hand that only sought to love and care
The hand that rescued Peter from drowning in the sea
Was soon to feel the cross that it would bear

The hand that was tied up for the love that it had shown
The hand that didn't resist the enemy
The hand that didn't scream as the blunt pins held it high
With fingers reaching out to victory

The hand that couldn't die now writes the book of life
This hand also shares the bread and wine
And Jesus says, "Christian if you want to worship me
Just come and kiss this hand of mine."

Ian Smale

FINGERPRINTS

Jeremiah 1:5

Before I formed you in the womb I knew you, before you were born I set you apart.

Ink pads or finger paints; paper; pens.

God knows everything about us. He has made us all different. Even our fingerprints are different. Encourage everyone to make a fingerprint using an ink pad or finger paints and write their name and the prayer beside it. Compare and comment on everyone's different fingerprints. Hold out hands in front, touching fingertips together as you pray the prayer.

If you have already done the activity time option above, scan some of the clearer fingerprints into a PowerPoint display. Alternatively, if you have the equipment, *and with their permission*, photograph everyone as they arrive and then project the photos up on screen. Otherwise, encourage everyone to look carefully at the people around them. Comment on the differences between each other. Our personalities and mannerisms are different, too. Each of us has a unique value to God. Hold out hands in front, touching fingertips together as you pray the prayer.

Heavenly Father, thank you that you have made me unique and special. Amen.

On my tip toes I am tall
When I crouch down I am so small
I stretch my hands out then I'm wide
Jesus made me special
Jesus loves me when I'm tall
Jesus loves me when I'm small
Jesus loves me when I'm wide
Jesus made me special.

Ian Smale

GOD THE POTTER

Isaiah 64:8

Yet, O Lord, you are our Father. We are the clay, you are the potter; we are all the work of your hand.

Play dough or air-hardening clay.

Invite each person to model a cupped hand from a lump of play dough or air-hardening clay. Then ask them to make a small model of themselves and lay it in the cupped hand. Models can be taken home as a reminder that we are in God's hands, for him to shape.

Give everyone a lump of air-hardening clay to form into a small model of themselves. Invite them to lay it in their cupped hands as they consider the influences that mould us in ways that are not pleasing to God, and as the prayer is said. Models can be taken home as a reminder that God is at work in our lives.

Heavenly Father, thank you that you mould us into the people you want us to be. Help me to be open to be shaped and moulded only by you. Amen.

Like a stone, you break my hardness
Like a fire, You melt me down
Like a summer rain, you gently fall
Wash me deep into the ground.
Then like a clay, you take and form me
Like the sun, that brings the dawn
Like a breath of life, you breathe on me
I am born, I am born.

Ian Smale

IDEA 49

MY FOOTSTEPS

Psalm 119:133
Direct my footsteps according to your word; let no sin rule over me.

Paper; scissors; pen; glue.

Give each person six sheets of paper. They draw round their left shoe or foot on three sheets and their right shoe or foot on the other three. Cut out the six footprints and write on each one of the following six Bible verses: Psalm 25:4; 43:3; 48:14; 121:3; Proverbs 4:11–12; Isaiah 58:11. (If you have young children, print and photocopy the verses onto slips of paper for them to stick on their footprints.) God has a plan for each of our lives. He knows which direction we should take. We can find out his best way by asking him, listening to him and reading his word in the Bible. Lay out the footprints and step on each in turn as the verses are read out.

Before your meeting, prepare six footprints, each with a Bible verse, as above; copy at least enough of the footprints for everyone to have one; cut them out. Ask for volunteers to randomly spread the footprints about your meeting space. As they do that, encourage everyone to think about how God directs them. Is he like a Sat Nav, sometimes unpredictable and mysterious, or can he be trusted to guide us in his right, best way? Now ask the volunteers to move the footprints into an orderly path, right, left, right, left. . . as you read out the six verses. Invite people to journey around the path as you pray together.

Direct my footsteps according to your word Lord; let no sin rule over me. Amen.

Lord direct my footsteps according to your word
And let no sin rule over me
Lord help me to live by the gospel I've heard
And let no sin rule over me
And let no sin rule over me
And let no sin rule over me
Lord direct my footsteps according to your word
And let no sin rule over me

Ian Smale

PRAISING HANDS

Psalm 63:4
I will praise you as long as I live and in your name I will lift up my hands.

Sheets of plain paper, pen, scissors, frieze paper; washable felt pens in a range of colours.

When we tell God how great and wonderful he is, that's called 'praise'. Share with each other some ways that you think God is great. Invite each person to draw round their hands on the plain paper and write or draw ways they can praise inside their outline. Now cut round the hand shapes. Lifting our hands up to God is just one way of showing our praise. You can wave your paper hands in the air as you sing together.

Fix frieze paper to the wall with the prayer written in large letters in the centre. Invite everyone to come and draw round their hand on the frieze and write in a prayer or something to praise God for, making their contribution as colourful as possible. Alternatively, have a few children drawing round their hands and adults writing up the ideas as people call them out.

Heavenly Father, I want to praise and thank you every day. Amen.

I will praise you as long as I live
And in your name I will lift up my hands
I will praise you as long as I live
And in your name I will lift up my hands
I will praise you as long as I live
And in your name I will lift up my hands
For you are awesome O God
Let's sing praises to God
Let's sing praises to God
Let's sing praises to God our king
For God is the king
For God is the king
For God is the king of everything.

Ian Smale

IDEA 51

RUNNING WITH GOD

Psalm 18:29
With your help I can advance against a troop; with my God I can scale a wall.

Roll of wallpaper that looks like bricks; marker pens; cardboard boxes.

Talk about things that make it hard, or stop us, following Jesus e.g. friends who don't believe in God, too much time doing other things, questions about God, wanting my own way, etc. Write those things on the sides of cardboard boxes. Make a wall of boxes. Look at the wall together and ask if children want to follow Jesus even though those things are in the way. Pray the prayer and knock down the wall. Depending on numbers, do the prayer activity several times, building up the wall again for another group to knock it down.

Encourage everyone to think of things that make it hard, or stop us, following Jesus. Have volunteers write those things across the bricks of the wall. Have two people firmly hold the roll of paper at each end and repeat the prayer together. Ask for two or three volunteers to run at the wall together, bursting through it. If you wish, make several walls in different parts of your meeting space.

Heavenly Father, please help me to break through all the barriers that are stopping me from following you. Amen.

Check Psalm 18 verse 29
With help from God
Things will be fine
I can run through a troop
And scale a wall
And nothing on earth
Can make me fall
No nothing
No nothing
No nothing on earth
Can make me fall
With God's help
Nothing can stop me at all.

Ian Smale

SANCTUARY

Exodus 25:3–8 (Read the long list of objects and colours).

Fabric in different colours and textures that portray themes (e.g. blue, purple or white for the nativity, green for epiphany and trinity, purple for lent, red for Holy Week and Pentecost, white for Easter, gold for Ascension, calico or canvas to signify the wilderness, hessian or sackcloth to signify repentance); candles and matches; small wooden cross; rugs or floor cushions; background music; other objects to focus on themes (e.g. a rock to signify hard times, polished coloured stones or glass beads to represent precious blessings).

Long ago in Bible times, God told his people to make a special place for him and fill it with beautiful things. And they did. When it was finished, God said he would meet them there. And he did. Now, God lives in us by his Holy Spirit, but we can still make a time and place where we can quietly love and honour him. Play the music and involve everyone in preparing a sanctuary for God. Invite everyone to choose a place in the sacred place to sit. Light the candles. Read a Psalm, leave time for quiet reflection and finish with the prayer and song.

A sacred space or prayer station is simply an area set aside, allowing people to connect with God. Sometimes objects, symbols or texts can help us focus on a particular theme or signify prayer points. Invite people to bring along some objects or prepare a space as above. Either give time in your group meeting to use the Sacred Space or invite people to use it afterwards for reflection and prayer.

Dear Lord, please inspire me to be more creative in my prayer life. Amen.

Be still and know that God is here
God is here, God is here
Be still and know that God is here
God is here, God is here.

We worship you O Lord
We worship you
We worship you O Lord
Lord we worship you.

Ian Smale

IDEA 53

SHEEP

John 10:27–28

My sheep listen to my voice; I know them, and they follow me. I give them eternal life, and they shall never perish; no-one can snatch them out of my hand.

Cross stitch fabric; blue, purple and red embroidery wools; embroidery needles; scissors, pencils.

In Bible times a shepherd knew all his sheep by their different bleeting. He never left them, and would even lie down in the gateway of the sheep pen at night to protect them from wild animals. Jesus said he is our Good Shepherd. He knows us by name and takes care of us always. There are lots of references to embroidery in the book of Exodus. The priests' garments were to be decorated in blue, purple and scarlet threads. Give everyone a square of cross stitch fabric and ask them to draw the letters of their first name lightly on the fabric with a pencil. Use different coloured wools to embroider their name. (If you have young children they could make a sheep picture sticking cotton wool on thin card during this activity time.)

These days farmers often mark their sheep with dye so they will know which are theirs. In Bible times shepherds knew all their sheep. Give everyone three lengths of wool in red, white and blue and invite them to plait the strands and use them as a Bible bookmark as a reminder that Jesus, our Good Shepherd, knows us by name, and has marked us with his Holy Spirit.

Lord Jesus

Thank you that you are the Good Shepherd and you take care of us. Amen.

Jesus said he's like a shepherd
Jesus said we are like sheep
And the sheep who listen to his command
Can never be snatched from within his hand
Can never be snatched from within God's hand
It says in John ten, twenty-nine:
'You will live forevermore
I know your name and you are mine.'

Ian Smale

SHIELD OF FAITH

Ephesians 6:16

Take up the shield of faith, with which you can extinguish all the flaming arrows of the evil one.

Roman soldiers in battle carried a huge shield in front of them. They marched shoulder to shoulder, their shields linked together, to prevent enemy arrows and weapons getting through. The Bible says that Christians carry a shield of faith to protect us against temptation and evil. Being close together and sharing our battles helps us all keep safe. Invite everyone to form lines with arms linked, and march forward singing the song. Finish with a battle cry e.g. God is our protector!

Roman soldiers in battle formed an interlocking shield, not for defence alone, but a means of rhythmic marching forward, shoulder to shoulder, thoroughly protected. Ask people to get into groups of five or six. Groups can consider how many battles are fought alone, and lost. Can sharing battles and marching forward together bring more victories? Share a few prayer requests within the group and then stand in a circle, arms linked, to pray.

Lord, as we put on our armour and lift up our shields of faith together, protect us please. Amen.

Put on the sword of the Spirit
Ba, ba, ba, ba, baa,
Ba ba baa ba baa
ba ba baa ba ba ba ba

The helmet of salvation

The belt of truth

The shield of faith

The breastplate of righteousness

And the shoes of the gospel of peace.

Ian Smale

SHOWING EMOTIONS

Psalm 139:14

I praise you because I am fearfully and wonderfully made.

Demonstrate body postures, asking everyone to guess how you feel e.g. hunched up – sad, grumpy, afraid; sitting with chin in hand – thinking; dancing around – happy, etc. However we feel, God knows and understands. Ask everyone to get into pairs. Instruct one of each pair to strike a pose that shows how they are feeling right now. Then they should tell their partner how they think God would like them to feel and their partner moves them into a new pose to show that feeling. Change places and repeat. Everyone should strike their second pose as you say the prayer.

Prepare in advance with several pairs of volunteers, possibly from your drama or dance group. Have one of each pair take an emotion, e.g. happy, sad, thoughtful, in pain, worried, burdened, confused etc, and frame that feeling physically, using their whole body. Ask people to guess the emotions. Read the Bible verse. Have the partners change the body positions into the opposite emotions. Read the Bible verse again. However we are feeling God wants us to praise him using all that we have and all that we are.

Dear Lord, please help me to express to you how I truly feel and to be open for you to change me. Amen.

I raise my hands up high
I bow my head down low
Then I kneel before the Lord
And say I love you

I raise my hands up high
I bow my head down low
Then I kneel before the Lord
And say I love you

Ian Smale

STRENGTH

Psalm 18:34

He trains my hands for battle; my arms can bend a bow of bronze.

Set of home gym weights; clippers; strong cotton; sticky tape; scissors; for each person – strong card 7.5cms x 10cms; lengths of silver, copper or green garden wire.

Make wire sculpture crosses:

- Wind the wire round the card three times horizontally and three times vertically to represent Father, Son and Holy Spirit.
- Finish off by winding round the centre of the cross diagonally.
- Make a small stand out of an extra piece of wire or use the cotton to add a hanging hook to the top of the card.

Invite everyone to think of a place to keep the cross as a reminder to stay strong in battle for God.

Show how to lift and hold weights sensibly. Work out some simple routines for volunteers to try. Lifting weights is one of the ways we can get stronger. The Bible tells us that God can make us strong to battle to do right and stay faithful to him. Hand out card and wire for everyone to fashion their own cross as above.

Thank you Lord for giving me the strength I need each day. Amen.

The Lord gives strength x 2
To those he loves x 2
He blesses them x 2
With peace x 2

According to his power
That is at work within us
According to his power
That is at work within us.

The hand of the Lord x 2
Will help the weak x 2
The arm of the Lord x 2
Gives strength x 2

According to his power
That is at work within us
According to his power
That is at work within us.

God is able to do x 2
A lot, lot more x 2
Than all we could ask x 2
Or Imagine x 2

According to his power
That is at work within us
According to his power
That is at work within us.

Ian Smale

IDEA 57

THE BODY

Ephesians 4:16

From him the whole body, joined and held together by every supporting ligament, grows and builds itself up in love, as each part does its work.

String puppet(s); card; scissors; split pins; paper; illustrated encyclopaedia.

Draw a simple body part template (body, head with neck, arm with hand, leg with foot). Copy onto card. Every part of our bodies is important, helping to make them work properly. Together, look at pictures of the human body in the encyclopaedia, pointing out supporting ligaments, muscles and joints. Everyone can work together to cut out body parts and assemble them with split pins into lots of people holding hands. (If you have a large number of young children you may prefer to make rows of people holding hands by concertina folding sheets of paper; drawing a simple figure on the front with arms reaching the folded edges; cutting round the figure through all thicknesses, leaving the folds intact where the arms reach the edge and then unfolding the string of people.) How is the church like a body?

Invite volunteers to come and attempt to make your string puppet(s) stand, walk, sit and lie down. Have everyone stand up and consider how they did that – decision, nerve cells and brain synapses carrying messages to muscles, ligaments, sinews, joints, and eyes and ears giving balance. Every part is important, including our support systems. Invite everyone to join hands as you pray, sing and reflect on how the church is the body of Christ.

Dear Lord, please help me to support my family and friends. Amen.

I'm part of a body
Not just any body
I'm part of the body of Jesus
I'm part of a body
Not just any body
I'm part of the body of Jesus

All alone I cannot be
When I've the church
Surrounding me
I'm part of a body
Not just any body
I'm part of the body of Jesus

Ian Smale

THROW CARES AWAY

1 Peter 5:7
Cast all your anxiety on him because he cares for you.

Brightly coloured paper; pens; waste paper bins.

What things get thrown away to be recycled? The rest of our rubbish is buried or burned, and we never see it again. The Bible tells us that Jesus loves us and wants us to hand our worries and concerns over to him. He won't recycle them and send them back. Ask everyone to write some of their worries on brightly coloured paper (hand out equal numbers of sheets of each colour of paper). Screw up their worries into a ball and then get into a team with all the other people with the same colour paper. Stand everyone in a wide circle with a large bin in the centre (allow young children to stand a few paces inside the circle). On your signal everyone throws their paper ball at the bin. The winning team is the one with the most balls in the bin.

Encourage everyone to consider their worries and concerns. Hand out sheets of paper for people to write some of their worries on. Find the Bible verse together and remind everyone that Jesus wants us to hand these things over to him. We can trust him to deal with them. Display and read the prayer as volunteers take the bins round and everyone screws up their paper and throws their worries in the bin.

Please God take my worries away.
I trust you to take good care of me. Amen.

Tell Jesus about all your worries, because he cares for you
Tell Jesus about all your worries, because he cares for you
Read 1 Peter 5 verse 7
And you'll see this is true
Tell Jesus about all your worries, because he cares for you.

Ian Smale

TRUST IN GOD

Acts 3:6

Silver or gold I do not have, but what I have I give you. In the name of Jesus Christ of Nazareth, walk.

You will need:

US dollar bill; thin paper cut to the size of the dollar bill; pens.

Take a US dollar bill with the words 'In God We Trust' written on it and pass it around for everyone to read. When the beggar man who couldn't walk saw Peter and John at the temple, he thought they would give him some money. They trusted in God and gave him something much better. With God's power the man jumped up and walked. Design your own bank note with 'Trust in God' written on it.

Pass around the dollar bill, noting the inscription. The beggar man at the temple gate looked to Peter and John for money but with their trust in God they gave him so much more. Encourage everyone to think of someone they know who is trusting God for something important. They can intercede on their friend's behalf.

Dear God, please help me to trust you more. Amen.

Song:

Trust in God with all your heart
Trust in, trust in God
Trust in God with all your heart
With all your heart, trust in God
Trust in, trust in God.

Trust in God with all your friends

Trust in God with all your health

Trust in God with all your life.

Ian Smale & Suzy Mills

WASHING HANDS

Psalm 24:4a, 5a

He who has clean hands and a pure heart. . . will receive blessing from the Lord.

Rosy apple; skewer; black ink or paint; knife; bowl of water; towel.

In advance, bore a narrow hole with a skewer right down into the centre of the apple through the stalk join. Carefully pour in some black ink or paint. Clean and polish the apple. Invite volunteers to come forward to have a piece of apple, then cut it open. The Bible tells us that our sin and bad thoughts are like this apple. Whatever we do we can't make ourselves clean inside. Only Jesus can wash us clean. When we've asked Jesus to do that, every time we wash our hands we can remember that Jesus has made us clean. Ask everyone to wash their hands and repeat the prayer after you.

Provide space for reflection. Have our hands conducted good deeds? Have our hearts stayed pure throughout all conversations, TV and internet viewing, relationships at work, the business of the week? It's all too easy to become soiled and unclean. Now is a time for Jesus to renew, cleanse, refresh. As a symbol, invite everyone to wash their hands and pray the prayer below.

Dear Lord Jesus, thank you for dying for me on the cross and making me clean inside. Amen.

If you have clean hands and a pure heart
You will receive blessing from the Lord
If you have clean hands and a pure heart
You will receive blessing from the Lord

You ask me how I can be sure
Jesus died on the cross to make me clean and pure

If you have clean hands and a pure heart
You will receive blessing from the Lord.

Ian Smale

TASTE

IDEA 61

BREAD

Matthew 26:26

While they were eating, Jesus took bread, gave thanks and broke it, and gave it to his disciples saying, "Take and eat; this is my body."

Different kinds of bread; baskets or trays; dips.

Two kinds of bread were made in Bible times: wheat bread and barley bread. Wealthy people mostly ate wheat bread and poor people ate barley bread. The bread that the boy gave Jesus to be multiplied was probably made from barley, and it fed five thousand people. Bread was usually baked in three different forms. There were smaller loaves like our bread rolls. There were large, round-shaped loaves and there was flat bread made without any leaven or yeast. That kind of bread was used to scoop up food and dip into sauces. Show and talk about the different breads we have today. Break them into pieces and share round with the dips.

Invite volunteers to name the different cereals used for making bread e.g. corn, wheat, rye, barley, oats, millet, etc. Today we have bread made from a variety of cereals but in Bible times there were mainly only two kinds used for making bread: wheat and barley. Wheat bread was usually eaten by wealthier people, and poorer people ate barley bread. Jesus said that when we break bread and eat it we are to remember that his body was willingly broken for us. Break up the various kinds of bread and invite everyone to try them.

Dear Lord

Thank you for your body which was broken for us. We give our bodies back to you to be a living sacrifice. Please take our bodies and use us to do your work and to glorify your name. Amen.

5000 plus hungry folk (x 3)
Came 4 2 listen to Jesus.

The 6 x 2 said 000 (x 3)
Where can I get some food from?

Just 1 had 1 2 3 4 5 (x 3)
Loaves and 1 2 fishes.

When Jesus blessed the 5 plus 2 (x 3)
They were increased many times over.

5000 plus 8 it up (x 3)
With 1 2 3 4 5 6 7 8 9 10 11 12 basketsful left over.

Ian Smale

FIGS

Micah 4:3b – 4

They will beat their swords into ploughshares and their spears into pruning hooks. Nation will not take up sword against nation, nor will they train for war any more. Every man will sit under his own vine and under his own fig tree, and no-one will make them afraid, for the Lord Almighty has spoken.

Pens; paper; baskets; fresh, ripe figs; fig roll biscuits; black paper; chalks; green fabric.

Supply pens and paper. If peace had a taste, what do you think it would taste like? Invite everyone to write out their ideas and place them in a basket. Read them out and see if everyone can guess who made which choice. Figs were used for food and medicine in Bible times but were also a sign of peace and prosperity. The Hebrew word for fig is *teenah* meaning to spread out, and it was the custom for people to sit peacefully under the shade of a spreading fig tree. Where is your fig tree, figuratively speaking? Imagine yourself there now and ask for God's peace for yourself and for the world. If the weather is fine and you have trees outside, sit under them with some fresh figs and enjoy their sweet taste as you pray. Children might prefer some fig roll biscuits. They could draw a peaceful picture with the black paper and chalks.

Lay bowls of figs or fig roll biscuits on green fabric at the front in a large space. If not in season you could use dried figs or the tinned variety. In Bible times figs were used for medicine and food but were also a sign of peace and prosperity. The Hebrew word for fig is *teenah* meaning to spread out, and it was the custom for people to sit peacefully under the shade of a spreading fig tree. Where is a good place for you to be at peace, and to pray for peace? Invite people to come and taste the figs and to pray. The green fabric is a symbol of the green fig leaves.

Heavenly Father

Please help me to know your peace in my life and I pray for peace throughout the world. Amen.

As the fiery sun shines bright, your love is warmth inside me,
As the crashing wave strikes shore, you remind me of your power;
As a mother feeds her young, you nurture and sustain me
In my father's loving arms, I know I am secure.

And there's nothing in this world could come between us,
Hell itself will try, but it will not prevail;
For you will never leave me in this world to fight alone
And a promise from your lips can never fail.

As the night descends I sleep in peace that you alone can give,
As the eagle soars on high, I feel released and free;
As the wind blows wild and strong, my faith remains unshaken,
As a little baby cries, my every tear you see.

Ian Smale

IDEA 63

FISH

Matthew 4:18–20

As Jesus was walking beside the Sea of Galilee, he saw two brothers, Simon called Peter and his brother Andrew. They were casting a net into the lake, for they were fishermen. "Come follow me," Jesus said, "and I will make you fishers of men." At once they left their nets and followed him.

A4 sheets of plain paper cut into fish shapes with vertical slits every 1/2 inch; strips of coloured paper for weaving; paper; sequin shapes; crêpe paper; tin foil; glue; scissors; felt pens; prawn flavoured crisps.

Jesus called his disciples to be fishers of men and the kingdom of heaven is likened to a dragnet. In Jerusalem there was a Fish Gate through which the traders brought fish to sell. Fishermen needed to be physically strong and at least seven of Jesus' disciples were fishermen. The Bible mentions fishing by spear, hook, harpoon or net. The fishermen used small rowing or sailboats and fished at night. The most common methods of preparing fish to eat was by roasting, salting or drying. Using the fish shape and strips of paper weave your fish and decorate it. The crisps can be eaten while the fish are made. Who are the 'fish' you are currently praying for? Name them before God and pray for strength to not give up.

In advance cut out simple fish shapes. One of the symbols of Christianity is the sign of the fish from the Greek *ichthus,* which are the initial letters in Greek of the words *Jesus Christ God's Son Saviour.* Give one fish to each person and invite them to write the names of those they are currently praying for all over the fish shape. Fold up the fish and draw a heart shape on the outside. Pass around the fishy crisps.

Lord Jesus

I am following you. I am also a fisherman for you. Please help me to pray steadfastly for those I have named so that they will come to follow you too. Amen.

The disciples went fishing x 3
On the Sea of Galilee
The disciples caught nothing x 3
A sorry sight to see.

Jesus said to the disciples x 3
On the Sea of Galilee
Cast your nets the other side boys x 3
Just trust in me.

The disciples went fishing again x 3
On the Sea of Galilee
This time they caught buckets full
This time they caught nets full
This time they caught boats full
They were happy as can be.

Let's remember this story x 3
About the Sea of Galilee
If we do what Jesus tells us x 3
How exciting life will be.

Ian Smale

FRUIT

Galatians 5:22–23

But the fruit of the Spirit is love, joy, peace, patience, kindness, goodness, faithfulness, gentleness and self-control. Against such things there is no law.

Fruits mentioned in the Bible e.g. apples, figs, dates, grapes, melon, raisins, pomegranates; blindfold: PowerPoint display.

Gather together some of the fruits mentioned in the Bible. Blindfold each person in the group in turn and give them a piece of fruit to taste. See if they can guess which one it is. Each of us has around ten thousand taste buds and four tastes detected by the tongue: sweet, sour, salty and bitter, enabling us to enjoy our food. We sometimes lose our sense of taste while suffering a cold and know how boring food is without it. How amazing of God to give us taste!

Play the game above with a group of volunteers. Display a PowerPoint of fruits as you pray.

Heavenly Father

Thank you that you have made so many delicious fruits for us to feast on and enjoy. But please help us to show the fruit of your Spirit to others. Amen.

Love is joy and love is peace
Love is patience and kindness
Love shows goodness – what it is
Love of course is faithfulness
Love is also gentleness
And love is self-control.

Ian Smale

GRACE SO SWEET

2 Corinthians 12:9

My grace is sufficient for you, for my power is made perfect in weakness.

Thin, plain card or old greetings cards; paper; glue; scissors; pens; small sweets; a gift box holding sweets for distribution (if you need large boxes, cover cardboard boxes with bright wrapping paper).

Grace is a special gift from God. He loves us and gives us grace to help us live like Jesus. As a reminder of God's gift of grace, make special gift boxes:

- Copy the box template onto thin card.
- Cut out and score the fold lines.
- Glue or tape the four side tabs on the inside of the box.
- Decorate.

Either invite people to write out the prayer or have photocopies in outline font for young children to colour in. Put the prayer in the gift box with a few small sweets. Take your gift box home and enjoy one of the sweets each day. They will soon run out, but God's grace never will.

Invite everyone to take two or three sweets from your gift box. Challenge them not to eat any of the sweets they have taken, but to give them away to their friends and family as a sign of their love. (Some children will work out they can give them to each other to ensure they still have one to eat themselves!)

Dear Lord, thank you for the gift of grace.
Please help me to show grace and love to others. Amen.

It is by grace we've been saved, by faith;
It is by grace we've been saved, by faith.
It is by grace we've been saved
And through nothing we could do
It is the gift of God.

The Lord's grace is sufficient for us
The Lord's grace is sufficient for us
The Lord's grace is sufficient
And through nothing we could do
It is the gift of God.

The grace of God brings salvation to all
The grace of God brings salvation to all
The grace of brings salvation
And through nothing we could do
It is the gift of God.

Ian Smale

GRAIN

Matthew 12:1

At that time Jesus went through the cornfields on the Sabbath. His disciples were hungry and began to pick some ears of corn and eat them.

Popcorn, popped and unpopped; baskets; a fresh corn on the cob; microwave oven; PowerPoint display.

Raw grain picked from the fields is a lovely way to eat it, as the disciples knew when they did it themselves while walking with Jesus. In Bible times raw grain was also roasted in a pan and called ‘parched grain’. It was sometimes eaten with chunks of bread. Jesse told David to take this type of grain to his brothers (1 Samuel 17:17). Abigail gave roasted grain as a present to David (1 Samuel 25:18). Examine the unpopped corn and the corn on the cob. How many different cereals can you name? Make some popcorn to enjoy together, thanking God for all the cereals he provides for us to eat.

Create a PowerPoint display to include a modern agricultural harvest, a successful and a failed third-world harvest. Use the words of the prayer in your display. In Bible times, as now, good harvests were welcomed and needed. Leviticus 23 describes a special feast to celebrate the ‘First Fruits’ of the harvest. A sheaf of the first fruits had to be gathered and waved before the Lord. Men were specially appointed to go out and harvest the best sheaves. A crowd including children would gather round the field to show which ones were the best to harvest first. God has abundantly provided all that we need. What makes a harvest fail? What can we do to help people access God’s provision? Pass around the popcorn as people consider and pray.

Father God

Thank you for your provision of grain and cereals, plenty for all. Forgive us for not caring enough for those in desperate need of them. Please show us how to help. Amen.

The fields are ripe x 3
But where are the workers
Where are the workers
Where are the workers
To bring the harvest in?

Lord here am I x 3
And I want to be a worker
I want to be a worker
I want to be a worker
To bring the harvest in.

The fields are ripe x 3
And I am a worker
I am a worker
I am a worker
Bringing the harvest in.

Ian Smale

GRAPES

Deuteronomy 8:6–9

Observe the commands of the Lord your God, walking in his ways and revering him. For the Lord your God is bringing you into a good land – a land with streams and pools of water, with springs flowing in the valleys and hills; a land with wheat and barley, vines and fig trees, pomegranates, olive oil and honey; a land where bread will not be scarce and you will lack nothing.

Supple branches; wire; string; seedless grapes; a camera and printer or paper and pens; family photographs.

The grape vine is the first cultivated plant to be recorded in the Bible, grown for eating and wine making. There are three words translated as wine in the Old Testament: *yayin* meaning wine; *sekar* meaning strong drink and *tiros* meaning new or sweet wine. The last may have been unfermented (non-alcoholic) wine. The vine is the most honoured plant in Scripture and Jesus compared himself to the vine and his people to the branches. Construct a vine out of pliable willow branches, wire and string. Take and print photos of everyone or invite them to draw pictures of their family. Attach the pictures to the vine. You could also attach a few small bunches of grapes. As you pick some grapes to eat, look at the pictures of people attached to the vine and pray for them.

In advance, invite everyone to bring a family photograph or *with permission* take photos of people as they arrive and print them. Construct a vine as above where everyone can see it. Palestine was known for its heavy clusters of large juicy grapes. Sometimes one bunch could weigh up to eleven kilos and needed two men to carry it on a pole. The grapes were grown for eating and making wine of various kinds. Vines are cut back severely after each season. They grow prolifically again, their branches trained to produce the best grape harvest. Jesus would have watched skilled vine workers who knew when to prune and how to train vines to grow productively. He compared himself to the vine and those who belong to him as the branches. Collect up photographs and pictures or invite everyone to come and fix them to the vine, pray for the people and sample the grapes.

Dear Lord Jesus
You are the vine and we are the branches. Please help us to stay well and truly attached to you and each other, and help us please to bear fruit. Amen.

Taste and see that God is good
Experience this brand new wine
Come and eat of the living bread
Be grafted to the living vine.
Then as you receive you will find
Hell itself can't undermine – the truth
You'll never be parted from the love of Jesus.

Ian Smale

HERBS

1 Peter 1:24–25

"All men are like grass, and all their glory is like the flowers of the field; the grass withers and the flowers fall, but the word of the Lord stands forever."

Packets of familiar herb seeds; cardboard egg boxes; compost; cut herbs e.g. rosemary, thyme, mint, chives, basil, lemongrass, etc.; paper; pens.

People who lived in Jesus' time were wonderful herbalists and many herbal plants are mentioned in the Bible. People used herbs to flavour food and also as medicine, with recipes handed down from generation to generation. Show some cut, grown herbs and taste them. Split the egg boxes into sections to plant some seeds for everyone to take home and grow.

For centuries, many of our plants have been used for medicinal purposes, to aid digestion and to flavour food. Some herbs and plants mentioned in the Bible include dandelion, sorrel, hawkweed, sow-thistle, wild lettuce, mint, wormwood and chicory which grow abundantly in the peninsula of Sinai, in Palestine and Egypt. In Exodus 12:8 the Israelites were commanded to eat the Passover lamb 'with unleavened bread and with bitter herbs'. The bitter herbs were to remind them of the long, bitter years they had spent in Egypt. Strip the leaves from the herb stems. Place in separate, numbered containers. Invite volunteers to come and taste the herbs and guess what they are. Award packets of herb seeds for correct guesses.

Heavenly Father

Thank you that you created all things. Thank you for the herbs and plants that you created to give us pleasure and make us well. Amen.

Though the grass may wither
And the flowers may fall
The word of the Lord
Will stand forever
Though the grass may wither
And the flowers may fall
The word of the Lord
Will stand forever.

Ian Smale

HONEY

Psalm 119:103

How sweet are your words to my taste. Sweeter than honey to my mouth.

Jar of honey; bread; butter or margarine; knives; plates; PowerPoint display.

In Bible times a Hebrew boy would be welcomed on his first day at school by the Rabbi, his teacher. He would be shown a slate with the letters of the Hebrew alphabet carved on it in various combinations, and with two of the basic texts of the Law. The teacher read these sentences out to the boy and the boy would repeat them back. The slate was then smeared with honey, and the boy was allowed to trace the letters in the honey with his fingers and lick them afterwards. The Hebrews believed that learning Scripture should be fun and should be rewarded. Make honey sandwiches and pray inwardly as you eat them.

Create a PowerPoint display showing bees flying to and from the hive. Incorporate the prayer into the display. Make up small triangles of honey sandwiches. In Bible times honey was one of the few sweeteners available, and much prized. Children especially enjoyed it. Little children were given honey cakes to eat shaped in the letters of the Hebrew alphabet. Even long ago those people knew that taste is a powerful way to learn and so enjoyable. Show the PowerPoint display and pass around the sandwiches.

Thank you Lord for the Bible. Please help me to read, learn and enjoy all you have to tell me through your Word. Amen.

If I try and read a little bit o' Bible every day
If I ask the Lord to help me
I'll know just what he'll say, he'll say,
'If you try and read a bit o' Bible every day
You'll learn the truth that life is best
When living Jesus' way.'

Ian Smale

LAMB

Genesis 22:13–14

Abraham looked up and there in the thicket he saw a ram caught by its horns. He went over and took the ram and sacrificed it as a burnt offering, instead of his son. So Abraham called that place The Lord Will Provide. And to this day it is said, "On the mountain of the Lord it will be provided."

Unleavened bread; lamb; egg; salt; lettuce; charoset or marzipan.

Recreate the Passover Meal, explaining each symbolic component. Most libraries carry books that will give full details, and the children's library will have a simplified version with pictures for children you may have present. The Israelites celebrated Passover every year in families, remembering God's deliverance from Egypt. All the food shown, tasted and eaten symbolised what had happened to them.

Set up a table with all the components of the Passover Meal. Hold up all the elements of the meal in order, talk about them and invite volunteers to come and taste. In Jewish families, even today, the food is eaten in ritual order and its meaning and symbolism discussed. Psalms 113–118 were sung during the meal, and together everyone remembered again God's love and mercy towards them.

- *Matzot* is the unleavened bread which is eaten symbolically three times during the meal.
- A whole lamb was roasted as a sacrifice without a bone being broken. If a family was too small to eat all the meat, others would be invited to share the meal. When the Temple at Jerusalem was the centre of Jewish life, Jews would go there at Pilgrim Festivals to sacrifice a lamb or goat.
- A hard boiled egg was set on the table. Food usually becomes soft and digestible when cooked, but eggs become harder. So the hard boiled egg symbolises the Jews' determination not to abandon their beliefs under the oppression of the Egyptians.

- Greenery was usually wild lettuce to represent new life.
- Salt water represented the tears of a slave.
- Four cups of wine recall the four times God promised freedom to the Israelites, and symbolise liberty and joy.
- *Charoset* is a paste made of apples, nuts, cinnamon and wine, to represent the mortar used by the Israelites to build the palaces of Egypt.
- An extra cup of wine is placed on the table and the door is left open for Elijah. Jews believe that the prophet Elijah will reappear to announce the coming of the Messiah.

Heavenly Father

Thank you that you provided the way of salvation for us through your Son, the Lamb of God, Jesus Christ our Lord. Amen.

Jehovah Jireh – God will provide
Jehovah Rophe – God heals
Jehovah M'keddesh – God who sanctifies
Jehovah Nissi – God is my banner
Jehovah Rohi – God my shepherd
Jehovah Shalom – God is peace
Jehovah Tsidkenu – God our righteousness
Jehovah Shammah – God who is there.

Ian Smale

LEMON

Leviticus 23:40

On the first day you are to take choice fruit from the trees and palm fronds, leafy branches and poplars, and rejoice before the Lord your God for seven days.

Branches; strong thread; scissors; lemons; lemon sorbet; plates.

The Feast of Tabernacles or Booths was known as *sukkot*. It is the longest Jewish holiday, celebrates the ingathering of the harvest and remembers the Hebrew people's long wandering in the wilderness. They collected one palm branch *(lulav)*, two willow branches *(arayot)* and three myrtle branches *(hadassim)*, binding them together. The bundle, called the *lulav*, was held in one hand while an *etrog*, a citrus fruit similar to a lemon, was held in the other as a symbol of cleansing and new beginnings. The branches were then waved in six directions, east, south, west, north, up and down to symbolise God's presence everywhere, while prayers of blessings were recited. If possible, have a woodland walk together. Collect and bind branches. Wave them, thank God for a clean, fresh start and ask for his blessing on the families represented. Shelters can be made from branches. Let everyone taste segments of lemon or lemon sorbet.

The Feast of Tabernacles took its name from the custom of living in booths or tents during its seven-day festival. After the establishment of the Temple in Jerusalem, the tents were erected in open spaces around the city e.g. on rooftops, in the courts of houses, in the precincts of the Temple and outside the city walls in open countryside. Children decorated the tents with citrus fruits. It was the last of the three great annual festivals at which every man of Israel was required to appear before the Lord at the sanctuary.

In advance, fix a tree branch firmly into a plant pot and display. Cut lemons into slices. Invite children to come and fix slices of lemon to the branch and to pray the prayer aloud. Pass around more slices for everyone to taste.

Heavenly Father

Thank you for the harvest. Thank you for making us clean. Thank you we can praise you with branches and fruit and all of your creation. Amen.

Create in me a brand new heart
One that's clean and won't depart
From the laws that you impart
God of all creation.
Your word will blossom and will grow
The Spirit's fruit will start to show
Through my new life the world will know
You're the God of new creation.
All you made was good to see
Perfection was your guarantee
And now your Spirit's changing me
You're the God of recreation.

Ian Smale

MILK

Exodus 3:8

So I have come down to rescue them from the hand of the Egyptians and to bring them up out of that land, into a good and spacious land, a land flowing with milk and honey.

Ingredients for the milk and honey pie; cracker biscuits; creamy cheese; herbs; honey; knife; trays.

In Bible times milk was part of the staple diet. It was also used to make curds, butter and cheese. The rich pasture land in Canaan, flocks of animals and abundance of milk was a sign of prosperity. It was often given as a drink to welcome strangers, to accompany meals, and was sometimes mingled with honey and wine as a rich delicacy. Milk was also used in the Bible as a metaphor for nurturing people on the word of God or the law. Make the milk and honey pie and encourage everyone to try it.

To make the pie you will need:

- 22cm pastry case
- 450g creamy goat's milk cheese
- 115g honey
- 6tbsp caster sugar
- 3 eggs lightly beaten
- 1 tsp vanilla essence
- ground cinnamon
- icing sugar

Pre-heat the oven to 175°C / 350°F / Gas mark 5. Mix the cheese with honey, add the sugar, eggs, and vanilla, and a sprinkling of cinnamon. Bake the mixture in the pastry case for 30–35 minutes. Top with some seasonal berries and sprinkle with cinnamon and icing sugar.

Milk was plentiful in Bible times, kept in skin bottles and served in bowls. It was quickly used each day and some made into cheese or curds because people had no means to keep it fresh. It was sometimes mixed with honey, wine or spices. The Bible also uses milk as a symbol of immaturity, being used for infants (Hebrews 5:11–14; 1 Peter 2:2–3). Prepare cracker biscuits with toppings of plain cream cheese, mixed with honey or various herbs, and place on trays. Pass around the trays of crackers and cheese.

Thank you Lord for milk and honey, symbols of your providence and goodness. Thank you also for your Word the Bible which nourishes us spiritually. Amen.

Thank you Lord for the food that's before me
Thank you Lord it sure looks great.
Thank you Lord for the hands that prepared it
I'll eat it up (you'll eat it up) I'll eat it up
And leave a clean plate.

Ian Smale

MUSTARD SEED

Matthew 17:20

I tell you the truth, if you have faith as small as a mustard seed, you can say to this mountain, 'Move from here to there' and it will move. Nothing will be impossible for you.

Packets of mustard seed; containers; compost; small cards; sticky tape; trays; flip charts; felt pens.

Both in Bible times and today mustard is used to flavour food. In Palestine both black and white mustard grew wild usually to about 4 feet or more. Black mustard was also cultivated in gardens for its seed which was used as a condiment and oil. Jesus used the mustard seed as an example of how our faith and the kingdom of God grow from tiny beginnings. Pass around the mustard seeds and taste them. Try planting some in small containers, to be transplanted in a garden if they grow.

The expression mustard seed was often used by the Jews as a metaphor for anything minute. Through the incarnation of Christ, his death and resurrection the kingdom of God was said to have been established. At the time this event was treated as insignificant by much of the known world. Yet since then the Jesus Movement has continued to grow and flourish as people everywhere find salvation through Christ and faith in God. In advance, cut small lengths of sticky tape and fix to tray edges. Pass around trays of mustard seed, cards and sticky tape. Invite everyone to take just one seed and fix it to the card with sticky tape. Has your faith grown from its tiny beginnings? Are you strong, spreading branches to give shelter and support to others? Are you bearing fruit and seed? Do you pray big prayers with faith? Give time for reflection and encourage everyone to put their seed card in a prominent place to inspire personal growth and faith. Invite children to the front to taste the seeds and to draw large pictures of mustard plants.

Dear Lord
As I look at these tiny mustard seeds help me to grow in faith and to believe that you will answer my prayers. Amen.

Jesus said, 'If you have faith
As small as a mustard seed,
You can say to this mulberry tree
Be uprooted and planted in the sea,
Uprooted and planted in the sea, sea,
See it obey you.'
Luke seventeen verse six confirms
What a little faith can do.

Ian Smale

IDEA 74

OLIVES

1 Kings 17:15–16

She went away and did as Elijah had told her. So there was food every day for Elijah and for the woman and her family. For the jar of flour was not used up and the jug of oil did not run dry, in keeping with the word of the Lord spoken by Elijah.

Ingredients for olive and barley bread; olive oil spread; olives; trays.

Olives and bread were part of the staple diet in Bible times. Olives were a symbol of peace, beauty, strength, divine blessing and prosperity. The fruit of the olive tree in its wild state grows fairly small and is worthless. To become prolific the olive tree must be grafted and cultivated. In advance, make some olive and barley bread as below to the point where it has doubled in size. Finish making the bread together and when cool invite everyone to spread with hummus or olive oil spread.

To make the bread you will need:

- 1 cup barley flour
- 1 cup rye flour
- 1 cup chickpea flour
- 1 cup wholemeal flour
- 1 cup caraway seeds
- 1 cup pitted and chopped olives
- 2 tsp active dry yeast
- 1 tsp baking soda
- a tsp salt
- 2 cups sour milk
- 1/2 cup warm water
- 8 tbsp olive oil

Dissolve the yeast in warm water. Stir the sour milk into the baking soda. Combine the flours in a mixing bowl with the salt, add the yeast mixture, milk and olives. Toss in the caraway seeds, then knead by hand for about 10 minutes. Cover the bowl with clingfilm and let the dough rise in a warm place for about 2 hours, or until doubled in size. Turn the dough out onto a heavily floured board and knead for a few minutes, then divide it into 16 equal portions, rolling it into balls. Flatten each ball into a small circle about 15cm in diameter, cover with a damp cloth and let sit for about 20 minutes. Heat a frying pan to medium-high heat, add a few tablespoons of olive oil and put one dough circle into the pan; press with the back of a spoon so that small bubbles form, as when cooking pancakes. Cook for 2 minutes on each side. Repeat until all circles are cooked.

Olives and bread were an important part of the Israelites' diet. To produce a good crop of olives a graft of a cultivated olive tree was inserted into the stem of a wild olive tree. The wild tree was cut down to the root to allow it to feed only the cultivated branch. Paul reversed this process when he wrote about the grafting of the wild branch of Gentiles onto the cultivated tree of the Jewish nation (Romans 11:24). In advance, make some olive and barley bread and break it into pieces. Provide olive oil spread, hummus and fresh olives of various kinds to accompany it. In groups, people can come to the table and try the bread and olives. Alternatively, pass around slices of bread and hummus.

Heavenly Father
Thank you for food and nourishment. And thank you that we are grafted into your family, the church, growing together in love like a healthy tree that bears good fruit. Amen.

My God shall supply all my needs x 3
Cos' it says so in the Bible
Cos' it says so where?
In the book that came from heaven
Cos' it says so where?
Isaiah fifty-eight eleven.
My God shall supply all my needs
Cos' it says so in the Bible.

Ian Smale

IDEA 75

POMEGRANATE

Exodus 28:33

Make pomegranates of blue, purple and scarlet yarn around the hem of the robe, with gold bells between them.

Fruits – grapefruit, orange, lime, lemon, pomegranate; pillow case; paper; pens; pomegranate juice; disposable cups; blue, purple and red finger paints, gold marker pens and frieze paper.

Put all the fruits in a pillowcase and give everyone thirty seconds to feel inside the pillowcase without looking, to try and identify the fruits. They can write their answers on paper and then compare afterwards. Show all the fruits, cut them open for tasting. Can you guess how many seeds are in a pomegranate? Jewish tradition says that there are six hundred and thirteen, one for each of God's commandments. Does anyone want to check? The pomegranate tree is small with lots of spreading branches. It is known as a very special or sacred tree and its fruit used as food, drink and medicine. The juice makes a refreshing drink. Grenadine syrup is made from the seeds, and medicine is made from the blossom. Pour out the juice for everyone to drink.

The high priests in the Old Testament period had pomegranates embroidered onto the hem of their robes. Not only has the pomegranate been revered through the ages for its medicinal properties, it also features in the heraldic crests of several medical institutions. A refreshing drink is made from the juice, a syrup called grenadine is made from the seeds and medicine made from the blossom. Pour out and share some pomegranate juice. Children present might like to finger-paint a frieze of pomegranates in blue, purple and scarlet and draw gold coloured bells in between whilst the drinks are passed round.

Heavenly Father

Thank you that you created all of these fruits for our pleasure and to heal us. As we drink this juice we pray for those we know who are ill, and ask you to heal them. Amen.

When you really understand
That God is your provider
Then reach out to Jesus
And by faith you will receive

Whatever God has said he'll do
Reach out and let him do it
Your Provider has provided
Believer just believe

I reach out and receive (x 3)
What God is doing
I reach out and receive (x 3)
What God is doing.

Ian Smale

IDEA 76

RAISINS

1 Samuel 30:12

They gave him water to drink and food to eat – part of a cake of pressed figs and two cakes of raisins. He ate and was revived.

Ingredients for raisin cake; raisins; bowls.

Share round mini-packs or bowls of raisins while telling the story. To keep safe from King Saul, David and his six hundred men had joined themselves to the Philistines under the patronage of the son of the king of Gath and they settled in the town of Ziklag. David attempted to fight with the Philistines against Israel but the Philistine commanders thought he planned to turn against them in battle, and sent him back to Ziklag. In their absence Ziklag had been raided and burned by the Amalekites and everyone taken away. After enquiring of the Lord what to do, David and his men pursued the raiding party. They came across an abandoned Egyptian slave of the Amalekites. He was in a bad way, but revived when given water to drink and fig and raisin cakes. His vital information led to a successful deliverance of David's people from the Amalekites.

In advance, make raisin cakes. Invite your drama group (if you have one) to create a dramatic presentation of David's adventures from 1 Samuel 29–30 with the Philistines, the attack on Ziklag and the deliverance of David's people from the Amalekites. While the presentation is in progress, pass around bowls of raisins or slices of raisin cakes.

To make raisin cakes you will need:

- 1 1/2 cups raisins
- 1 cup white granulated sugar
- 3/4 cup butter
- 2 tsp vanilla extract
- 1 tsp baking soda
- 1 1/2 cups SR flour

- 1 1/2 tsp ground allspice
- 2 tsp baking powder
- 2 cups water
- 1 tsp balsamic vinegar
- 3 eggs
- 1 1/2 cups oatmeal
- 1/2 tsp salt
- 2 tsp ground cinnamon
- 1 tsp ground nutmeg
- 1/2 cup chopped walnuts

Preheat oven to 175°C / 350°F / Gas mark 5. Lightly grease a 25cm square baking tin. In a large saucepan, boil the raisins in enough water to cover (about 2 cups), add the sugar and vinegar and stir. Set aside and let cool for about 10–12 minutes. To the same saucepan, add the butter, eggs, vanilla, and all the remaining dry ingredients and mix well. Bake for 35–45 minutes, or until a skewer comes out clean. Leave to cool and set then cut into squares.

Heavenly Father
Thank you for food that gives us energy and keeps us strong and healthy. Amen.

I'm not weary, I'm not faint
I'm an on fire overflowing thankful saint,
'Cause my Lord went to an enormous length
So I am able to renew my strength
And as I wait upon the Lord
I don't need to feel exhausted.
I just relax and face the facts
He gives my body what my body lacks.

Ian Smale

SALT

Matthew 5:13

You are the salt of the earth. But if the salt loses its saltiness, how can it be made salty again? It is no longer good for anything, except to be thrown out and trampled by men.

Black card; glue; rock salt crystals; small bowls.

The Israelites had an unlimited supply of salt from the Dead Sea. Salt was used not only to purify, preserve and flavour food but to seal agreements or covenants of faith and loyalty. In Numbers 18:19 and 2 Chronicles 13:5 the 'covenant of salt' is a symbol of eternity. Draw a cross shape on some black card. Cover the cross shape with glue. Now carefully sprinkle the salt crystals into the cross shape. The cross will become white and glistening in contrast with the dark background. Through his death and resurrection Jesus has made a covenant of love with us for eternity. Invite everyone to taste a few grains of salt.

Legal agreements, contracts, promises and covenants are solemn and binding. Breaking them can bring serious consequences. In Bible times covenants were sometimes made with salt, a symbol of eternity. Invite volunteers to make a large salt cross as above, where everyone can see it. Today it seems that agreements, contracts, promises and covenants can easily be broken or let-out clauses and other options found. The covenant Jesus made with us to deliver us from sin and bring us to God will never be broken. It's safe for all eternity. Pass around small bowls of rock salt crystals for everyone to taste.

Dear Lord Jesus

Thank you that you have covenanted to love me forever and ever. Amen.

Dear Lord
My Father who's in heaven
Honoured be your holy name
May your kingdom come
May your will be done
Here on earth
As it is in heaven

Dear Lord
Please give us food today
And forgive us
As we forgive others
May your testing be
Not too hard to bear
And deliver us from the evil one. Amen.

Ian Smale

SPICES

Genesis 43:11

Put some of the best products of the land in your bags and take them down to the man as a gift – a little balm and a little honey, some spices and myrrh, some pistachio nuts and almonds.

Spices; plates; plastic drink-stirrers; paper; pens; cinnamon biscuits; winter mixture or other sweets flavoured with spices; PowerPoint display; flipchart and pen.

Spices used in Bible times included balsam, cumin, cassia, cinnamon, calamus, coriander, dill, frankincense, galbanum, henna, myrrh, onycha, rue, saffron, spikenard and stacte. Some spices were used in food and some for anointing oil. Next time you go to the supermarket find the spices and count how many we have available to us today. Find six different jars of edible spices and make a small pile of each one on six plates. Label each plate with a letter of the alphabet. Give everyone six plastic drink-stirrers and paper and pen. Encourage spice sampling. The names of the spices can be written on the paper next to the letter of the alphabet. Compare answers. Share the cinnamon biscuits.

Display the names of the spices shown above on a PowerPoint illustrated with plants and herbs. In Bible times some of these spices were used to flavour food and some were used for anointing oil. Which spices do you recognise as ones we use today? What other spices do we use today? Write answers on the whiteboard. Put out six different edible spices on plates on a table and ask volunteers to taste and name them. Pass around the sweets.

Thank you Lord for all the different spices you have created to flavour our food and make it taste so good. Amen.

When you eat or drink or whatever you do
Do it all to the glory of God
When you eat or drink or whatever you do
Do it all to the glory of God
Life's to enjoy in so many ways
But never forget what the word of God says
When you eat or drink or whatever you do
Do it all to the glory of God.

Ian Smale

TASTE

Psalm 34:8

Taste and see that the Lord is good. Blessed is the man who takes refuge in him.

Ingredients for biscuits; pictures of food; or alternatively a packet of biscuits; PowerPoint display.

Follow the recipe below to make prayer biscuits. While the biscuits are cooking and cooling, show pictures of food and talk about foods and tastes that are disliked, and why. Ask what is good about knowing God.

To make the biscuits you will need:

- 150g SR flour
- 1/2 tsp bicarbonate of soda
- 100g sugar
- 100g margarine
- 1 egg
- 1 tbsp golden syrup;

Mix together the dry ingredients. Rub in the margarine, add the egg and syrup and knead the mixture into a soft dough. Cut into cross or heart shapes. Bake at 150°C / 300°F / Gas mark 4 for 5–10 minutes. Leave to cool on a wire rack.

Share the biscuits.

Invite several volunteers to list their favourite foods, and why they like them. Ask others to list their least favourite foods and why they dislike them. Alternatively, create a PowerPoint display of foods and conduct a poll of raised hands for the favourite and least favourite food. Divide the group into sections, or row by row, invite each group to call to the others, 'Taste and see that the Lord is good.' Pass around the biscuits and invite more volunteers to share their experiences of God's goodness.

Dear Lord

Thank you for the sense of taste, thank you for sweetness, thank you for these biscuits. Amen.

Behold I stand at the door and knock.
If any man hears my voice
And opens the door I will come into him
And eat with him and him with me.
And to him who overcomes
I will give the right to sit with me
On my throne just as I overcame
And am seated with my Father.

Ian Smale

WATER

John 4:13

Jesus answered, "Everyone who drinks this water will be thirsty again, but whoever drinks the water I give him will never thirst. Indeed, the water I give him will become in him a spring of water welling up to eternal life."

Buckets; water; a variety of flavoured bottled waters; plastic cups; trays; glass; cloth; towels.

Play this game outdoors or in a room that has a floor which can be mopped, alternatively use protective plastic sheeting. Place two empty buckets at one end of the room and two full of water at the other end. Divide into two teams. Have a relay race to see which team can fill their empty bucket from their full one the fastest – they can only use a plastic cup. All that chasing about makes us thirsty. There's nothing like a cool drink of water to refresh us. Share out the flavoured water and people can choose their favourite.

In advance, practise this trick! Place a piece of thin cloth over a glass and let it flop over the sides loosely. Pour in some water through the cloth until the glass is full. Ask a volunteer to help you. Stretch the cloth tightly over the glass, holding it down with one hand. Turn the glass upside down quickly. Hold it straight and the water will stay in. Pass around trays of flavoured water for everyone to sample.

Dear Lord Jesus

Thank you for giving us water. We pray for people today who have no clean water to drink and ask that you will provide for them. Amen.

For the Lamb at the centre of the throne
Will be their Shepherd
He will lead them to springs of living water
And God will wipe away
Every tear from their eyes
And God will wipe away every tear.

Ian Smale

SMELL

ALMOND

Exodus 25:33

Three cups shaped like almond flowers with buds and blossoms are to be on one branch, three on the next branch, and the same for all six branches extending from the lamp stand.

Fragrance-free (or faded) potpourri; large plastic bag; smaller paper gift bags or boxes; almond oil; bowl; air-hardening clay; PowerPoint display.

The Hebrew name for almond is translated as 'waker' meaning it is the first of the fruit trees to blossom after winter and a reminder that winter has passed. The blossom is pink and white and so beautiful that its shape is copied to decorate the furnishings in the Temple. As well as being fragrant and oil-producing it is also a favourite food. Gifts of almonds were given as delicacies in Bible times and today too. The almond is also a symbol of age.

Put the fragrance-free potpourri in a large plastic bag, without holes. Add drops of almond oil and shake well. Everyone can scoop some into smaller paper gift bags or boxes to seal to take home. If you have time everyone could make a bowl from air-hardening clay to keep their potpourri in at home.

Use PowerPoint to display some tree blossoms e.g. orange, cherry, almond, lilac, horse chestnut etc. Integrate the words of the prayer in the display. Fill a bowl with potpourri and scent it with almond oil. God has made some amazingly beautiful blossoms for us to enjoy. The almond tree blossom is so lovely and has such a sweet fragrance that God chose to use it to decorate the Tabernacle. Pass around the bowl of potpourri, inviting everyone to smell the fragrance as it passes by.

Thank You Lord for the beauty of your creation: for shape, colour and fragrance. Amen.

I'm looking up to Jesus
His face is shining beauty
I'm feeling so unworthy
Yet his Spirit leads me on

I'm looking up to Jesus
His radiance surrounds me
I feel so pure and clean
A taste of heaven on earth.

Ian Smale

ANOINTING OILS

Exodus 30:23–25

"Take the following fine spices: 500 shekels of liquid myrrh, half as much of fragrant cinnamon, 250 shekels of fragrant cane, 500 shekels of cassia – all according to the sanctuary shekel – and a hind of oil. Make these into a sacred anointing oil, a fragrant blend, the work of a perfumer."

Carrier oil e.g. grapeseed; two essential oils such as lavender and sandalwood, or buy them ready-made (choose oils that are gender specific or gender neutral). Alternatively, you could use several kinds of fragranced hand cream; tissues.

People and things were anointed in the Old Testament, to signify holiness or separation to God. People were also anointed to be kings and also for healing. Weapons were anointed for war, the Tabernacle and all the furnishings and priests' garments were anointed for service. Use the scented oils or add about twenty drops of your chosen essential oils to a 50ml bottle of carrier oil. Adjust for larger quantities. Let everyone shake the bottle and in pairs of prayer partners anoint each hand and pray together.

Add drops of essential oils to carrier oils (don't use essential oils directly on skin). Perfumed oils were used in Bible times to anoint objects or people as a sign of holiness or separation to God. The Tabernacle, and everything that God appointed to be in it, was anointed for service. Pass around the fragrant oils or hand cream. People can anoint the hands of the person next to them. As people smooth their hands together they can pray for healing for someone they know.

Dear Lord

As I anoint this person's hands with oil please bless them and keep them safe in your hands. Amen.

I worship you in holiness
I worship you in truth
I worship you in thankfulness
In the days of my youth
I worship you in gratefulness
For just being who you are
Lord in my own way
I just want to say – I love you.

I worship you in trembling
I see your enemies run
I worship you in wonder
I see the works you've done
I worship you in jubilance
You've fought the war and won
Lord in my own way
I just want to say – I love you.

I worship you the craftsman
The creator of all things
I worship you the mastermind
You've knowledge of all life brings
I worship you in majesty
You are the King of kings
Lord in my own way
I just want to say – I love you.

I love you Lord, I love you Lord
My Lord I love you.
I love you Lord, I love you Lord
My Lord I love you.
I love you Lord, I love you Lord
My Lord I love you.
Lord in my own way
I just want to say – I love you.

Ian Smale

BAKING

Leviticus 23:17

From wherever you live, bring two loaves made of two-tenths of an ephah of fine flour, baked with yeast, as a wave offering of firstfruits to the Lord.

Ingredients for making bread or part-baked bread.

The Jews believed in feasting and celebrating. There were three great annual festivals in the Jewish calendar, times of sacred joy and celebration, and other feasts in between. The Feast of Pentecost, also known as the Feast of Weeks or the Feast of Harvest was one of these. It was marked by the offering of the two wave-loaves. These were prepared from wheat grown in the best district of the country. God gave very precise details for the cutting of the grain, its thrashing, grinding and sieving to make the flour for this special bread, baked in the Temple itself on the evening before the festival. The loaves were long and flat in shape and turned up, either at the edges or at the corners, to represent the Ark of the Covenant. According to the *Mishnah* (the Jewish legal traditions orally handed down until they were compiled and written down in AD 200), each loaf was four handbreadths wide, seven long, and four fingers high, and the dough would weigh just over two and a half kilos. The wave-loaves were leavened to represent the ordinary food people ate. What a wonderful aroma of freshly baked bread must have spread through the Temple. Try baking some fresh bread and shaping it like the ark of the covenant or a cross, or use part-baked bread. Enjoy the smell and share the bread to celebrate God's powerful, holy presence with us.

God gave specific instructions to the Israelites for celebrating feasts and festivals. This helped them to remember that they were his chosen people, he had a plan for them and they were set apart for him. God instructed them to use ordinary materials that would be made holy by him. All his directions were filled with colour, music and sound, beautiful materials, wonderful food to taste and amazing aromas to smell. The wave-offering at the Feast of Pentecost may seem strange to us, but it was a meaningful and joyful celebration of God's faithfulness. How can we celebrate such faithfulness with everything we have and are? God has given us our senses so we can enjoy all that he has created for us. Bake fresh or part-baked bread. Share out the warm bread and encourage everyone to breathe in its appetising aroma.

Heavenly Father
Thank you for bread and cakes and the wonderful smell when they are baking. We gladly celebrate your faithfulness to us, your people. Amen.

Lord we've come to worship you
Lord we've come to praise
Lord we've come to worship you
In oh so many ways
Some of us shout
And some of us sing
Some of us whisper
The praise we bring
But Lord we all are gathering
To give to you our praise.

Ian Smale

CEDAR WOOD

Isaiah 41:19–20

I will put in the desert the cedar and the acacia, the myrtle and the olive. I will set pines in the wasteland, the fir and the cypress together, so that people may see and know, may consider and understand, that the hand of the Lord has done this, that the Holy One of Israel has created it.

Cedar wood oil; carrier oil; oil burner. In advance, put a few drops of the cedar wood oil into the carrier oil.

Cedar wood is a very fragrant wood known for its rich oil which has cleansing properties. The cedar wood that was used in Leviticus for ritual cleansing was a plant probably of the juniper family which gives off a strong fragrance when burnt. It is also known for its fragrance to help clear the head. *With permission,* touch everyone's forehead with the cedar wood oil. Ask God to clear away any thoughts that may be troubling people. Pray for his peace. Invite people to name others who are ill and need God's healing touch.

God has created some amazingly aromatic and sweet-smelling trees for us all to enjoy. To stand among them as a hot day draws to a close and breathe in their beauty is one of life's delights. Some trees also have healing and cleansing properties. When cedar wood is burned its strong fragrance clears the head. Put some cedar wood oil in an oil burner and as the fragrance fills the room pray and ask God to clear your mind from anything that might be troubling you and to heal anyone you know who is ill.

Heavenly Father

Thank you for your peace and your healing power. Amen.

How awesome are your deeds O Lord
How great is your power (x 2)
Your enemies fall before you (x 3)
So great is your power

The earth bows down to you O Lord
It sings its praise to you (x 2)
It sings its praise to your name (x 3)
So great is your power.

Ian Smale

FLOWERS

Matthew 6:28b–29

See how the lilies of the field grow. They do not labour or spin. Yet I tell you that not even Solomon in all his splendour was dressed like one of these.

Highly fragranced flowers in season e.g. rose, lily of the valley, jasmine, sweet peas, lilies, honeysuckle, lilac etc.; garden twine or cotton; blindfolds; pens; paper.

Blossom, plants and wild flowers grew in abundance during springtime in Palestine, mostly in the open fields and in the rich groves of trees around houses. Numerous kinds of wild flowers could be found in the plains and mountains as well. The almond had beautiful pink blossoms that the Israelites used as models for engravers to adorn the cups of the golden lamp stands. The camphire was a small plant or shrub that bore beautiful cream-coloured flowers that hung in clusters like grapes and were highly scented. It was used for orange dye. Cockle flowers were the purplish red flowers of a weed called the 'cockle' or 'darnel'. This plant grew abundantly in Palestinian grain fields. Its Hebrew name is spelled like the Hebrew word for "stink" and so is translated 'stinkweed'. The term 'lily' covered a wide range of flowers. The lily mentioned in Song of Solomon was a rare variety that had a bloom similar to a bright flame. The lily of the valley is known as the Easter lily. The lily mentioned in Hosea is more like an iris. The beautiful water lily or lotus was a favourite flower in Egypt and was used to decorate Solomon's Temple. The lilies of the field were probably a variety of colourful spring flowers such as the anemone. Gather different types of flowers and make up colourful bunches or bouquets either with mixed flowers or co-ordinated colours. Compare the scents. Write some prayer notes or texts and fasten onto the bouquets and give them away to family or friends.

Make small posies of highly scented flowers in advance and keep out of sight. Conduct a survey to see who buys flowers for someone every week, month, special occasions. God has blessed us with an abundance of flowers to enjoy in their natural habitat, and we can also enjoy them at home and in church. They are a constant reminder of God's goodness, super-abundance and a feast for our senses. Invite volunteers to be blindfolded and guess the identity of the unseen flowers from their aroma. Present winners with a posy. Encourage everyone to bless someone with an unexpected bunch of flowers or bouquet this week, accompanied by prayer and thanksgiving.

Heavenly Father
Thank you that you are the Creator God. Thank you for all the beautiful flowers, plants and fragrances you have made. Amen.

Don't worry about your life
Don't worry about what you eat
Don't worry about your life
Don't worry about what you drink

See the birds up in the air
They do not reap or sow
They do not store their food away
Yet Father God feeds them each day
And we are more valuable than they
Don't worry, trust God.

Don't worry about your life
Don't worry about how you look
Don't worry about your life
Don't worry about the clothes you wear.

Don't worry about your life
Don't worry about what tomorrow may bring
Don't worry about your life
Don't worry about anything.

Ian Smale

FRAGRANT OFFERING

Ephesians 5:1

Be imitators of God, therefore, as dearly loved children and live a life of love, just as Christ loved us and gave himself up for us as a fragrant offering and sacrifice to God.

Carrier oil e.g. almond or grapeseed; freshly cut rosemary; paper; pens; scissors; crêpe paper; string or wool.

In advance put rosemary cuttings into the carrier oil and leave for forty-eight hours. Cut the paper into A6 pieces (half A5). In the Old Testament we read about people making sacrifices to God for a whole number of reasons. One of the sacrifices or offerings was called the 'thank offering'. This is where people would give thanks to God and make a sweet sacrifice or fragrant offering.

Make a rosemary rope:

- Cut across folded crêpe paper to make streamers
- Join the streamers together
- Tie sprigs of rosemary along the streamers.

Think about something you would like to offer thanks to God for and write it on a piece of paper. Sprinkle the paper with the rosemary oil. As people are doing that have a couple of volunteers make their way past everyone holding and wafting the rosemary rope as they go.

We have so much to be thankful to God for. When children forget to thank us for a present it can be hurtful but many times we forget to thank God for things he gives us. The Bible tells us that thank offerings are a sacrifice to God. Offer the paper and pens and invite everyone to write their thank offering to God. Pass around the rosemary oil. Rosemary is known as a herb for remembrance. Sprinkle a few drops of the oil on what you have written to help you remember to be thankful. Keep it safe as a reminder of your thank offering.

Father God

We give you thanks today for all that you are, all that you mean to us and all that you have given us. We give you our praise and worship, our very selves. Amen.

Father God I wonder
How I managed to exist
Without the knowledge of your parenthood
And your loving care
But now I am your son
I am adopted in your family
And I can never be alone
'Cos Father God you're there beside me

I will sing your praises (x 3)
For evermore
I will sing your praises (x 3)
For evermore

Ian Smale

GARLIC

Numbers 11:5

We remember the fish we ate in Egypt at no cost – also the cucumbers, melons, leeks, onions, and garlic.

Ingredients for garlic bread or buy ready-made; trays or baskets.

There are over seventy different types of garlic and onion in Palestine. In Bible times garlic was used as a medicine as well as for flavouring food. It has a pungent smell, liked or loathed for its smell in equal measure. Bake some garlic bread from the recipe below, or buy it ready-made, to get the full effect of the aroma.

You will need:

- 1 baguette or ciabatta bread
- 3 large cloves of garlic
- 100g soft butter
- 2 tbsp flat-leaf parsley, chopped finely

Heat the oven to 200°C / 400°F / Gas mark 6. Peel and finely chop the garlic. Mix the chopped garlic with the butter and stir in the parsley. Make diagonal incisions in the bread about 3cm apart using a sharp knife. Use a knife to generously spread the garlic butter between the slices. Wrap the loaf in tinfoil and place in the middle of the oven. Bake for around ten minutes. For a crusted top, open the foil and bake for an extra five minutes.

The Hebrew people complained bitterly at God's amazing provision of food and longed for the variety of foodstuffs and flavours they had enjoyed in Egypt. All had been born there and although their heritage was elsewhere and they were slaves, they had known no other life. Now all had changed and, some of them thought, not for the better. Today we have the biggest variety of food ever available to people, in any season. We need to think carefully about responsible stewardship of the earth, but still remembering that God gives us all things to enjoy. If you have kitchen facilities available, bake the garlic bread then pass around slices while still warm.

Lord Jesus

Thank you for the senses of taste and smell. As we eat this bread we remember the complaints of the Israelites in the wilderness. Please help us to be grateful for food and not to complain. Amen.

Lord tell me your ways and show me how to live.
Lord tell me your ways and show me how to live,
Lord tell me your ways,
Show me how to live
Lord tell me your ways,
Show me how to live
Lord tell me your ways,
Show me how to live
Lord tell me your ways and show me how to live.

Ian Smale

GINGER

Song of Songs 4:13–14

Your plants are an orchard of pomegranates with choice fruits, with henna and nard, nard and saffron, calamus and cinnamon, with every kind of incense tree, with myrrh and aloes and all the finest spices.

Ginger biscuits, home-made or bought; root ginger; a selection of sweet-smelling herbs and spices.

The word for the plant calamus is derived from the Latin word for cane and it was a long reed-like plant. The leaves were a sweet-smelling cane or ginger grass which when crushed gave a lovely strong ginger smell. It was apparently imported from India for use in worship. There are several Hebrew expressions for 'calamus'. The basic Hebrew term *qaneh* means 'cane'. It is used in Exodus 30 as the word for balsam, referring to sweet cane or *cymbopogon*. In Jeremiah a similar plant is mentioned *qaneh tob* meaning either 'good' or 'perfumed'. Sweet cane and spices were used for their scent in Bible times and in particular for anointing oil. Give children a list of fruits and vegetables. Let people try to identify the different herbs and spices by smell.

Use this recipe to make some delicious ginger biscuits:

- 225g plain flour
- 100g margarine
- 100g sugar
- 2 tsp ground ginger
- 2 tsp baking powder
- 2 large tbsp golden syrup warmed
- 1/2 tsp baking soda

Dissolve baking soda in 1 tsp hot water. Sift the flour, ginger and baking powder into a bowl. Rub in the margarine. Add the sugar, then mix to a dough with the bicarbonate of soda mixture and syrup. Make walnut-sized balls and place them on greased baking sheets. Press down the centre of each ball with your thumb.

Bake in a preheated moderately hot oven 200°C / 400°F / Gas mark 6 for about 10 minutes.

Ginger was well known in Bible times, used in worship and for flavouring food. It gives a warmth and depth to food and aids digestion. Today we use the fibrous, knotty root of a creeping plant more used to the tropics for flavouring food, for digestion, to make warming teas to soothe and help clear head colds. Also good for travel and nausea. God is good, he knows what we need, and provides it for us. Peel and slice very thinly some ginger roots with a vegetable peeler. Pass around the ginger biscuits or raw slithers of ginger for brave people to taste! Alternatively, just inhale the aroma.

Dear Lord
As we smell the ginger and other aromatic plants and herbs may our prayers be a sweet offering to you. Amen.

The Lord is so cool (x 3)
He loves a child like me.
The Lord is mega (x 3)
He loves a child like me.
The Lord is awesome (x 3)
He loves a child like me.
The Lord is so cool
The Lord is mega
The Lord is awesome
He loves a child like me.

Ian Smale

HEALING OIL

James 5:14

Is any one of you sick? He should call the elders of the church to pray over him and anoint him with oil in the name of the Lord.

Bottles of olive oil; paper plates; oil pastels.

There was an abundance of olive trees in ancient Palestine and the oil was used for trade. Solomon supplied oil to Hiram as part payment for constructing the Temple. Oil was used in religious ceremonies like the firstfruits and meal offerings. It was used at the consecration of priests and the purification of lepers. It was used to light lamps and for cooking, instead of butter. It was used as a medicine and to heal bruises and wounds. It was used for bathing and for welcoming guests at a meal by pouring it over their head. Oil symbolised gladness, comfort, spiritual nourishment and prosperity.

Invite everyone to write down prayer words for healing on the paper plates, using the oil pastels e.g. fit, well, strong, healthy, calm, happy, etc. Then form a circle. Take some oil and rub it onto your hands. Take the person's hand on your right and pass on the oil to the left. As you pass on the oil pray for the person on your right.

Olives grew abundantly in ancient Palestine and were a profitable market product. Oil was an essential part of life and worship. It was used in the Temple and the home. Oil represented God's providence – people gladly shared it with strangers and guests. One of the many uses of oil was for anointing and in New Testament times James encouraged church leaders to pray for those who were sick in the name of Jesus, anointing them with oil. There may be people you know who are ill and need to be healed. Encourage them to ask for prayer for healing and to receive anointing from their church leaders.

Heavenly Father

Thank you that your word tells us we can pray for healing. We pray for those right now who need your healing. Lord of grace and glory, reach out to them now we pray. Amen.

Lord I strive but so often fail
Want to win but can't seem to succeed
Please pour out your mercy on me
I try to do your will
But there's so much to fulfil
As I take my eyes off me
I see your glory

I see your glory, God of grace, God of glory
I see your glory, God of grace, God of glory to me.

Lord I have such little faith
I'm silent when I know I should speak
Please pour out your mercy on me
I should be bold but I just feel fear
When you talk I don't seem to hear
But as I take my eyes off me
I see your glory.

Lord at times I am not real
Hold back when I know I should give
Please pour out your mercy on me
When tempted I sometimes fall
Am I any use at all?
But as I take my eyes off me
I see your glory.

Ian Smale

HYSSOP

Psalm 51:7

Cleanse me with hyssop, and I shall be clean; wash me, and I shall be whiter than snow.

Branches; buckets; water; hyssop or camphor oil; bubble wands; mint-scented shampoo; jam jars.

The Temple was sprinkled with branches of hyssop as a cleansing and purifying ritual. Hyssop is a member of the mint family along with the Judean sage. Hyssop is a fragrant wiry plant that grows up to three feet high. It has hairy branches and leaves and white, blue, pink or purple flowers. Because the stems are hairy they are able to hold water very well and useful for religious ceremonies and rituals that require sprinkling. Hyssop was used to sprinkle the doorposts of the houses in Egypt at the Passover. It was also used for cleansing lepers. It has since been discovered that the mould that produces penicillin grows on its leaves and would have given antibiotic protection to the lepers who were bathed in it. Make up solutions of mint-scented liquid soap in the jam jars. Let everyone have a turn at blowing mint-scented bubbles. As they do, pray and ask for cleansing and blessing.

The flowers and leaves of the hyssop plant can be used in cooking. When planted near cabbages it lures away cabbage-white butterflies. If planted near vines, it increases the yield. The flowering tops can be infused to ease throat and lung complaints and to aid digestion, and its essential oil soothes bruises. The ritual cleansing of the Temple with hyssop symbolised God's purity which is whiter than snow. Dip branches of hyssop, mint or similar plants in a bucket of water and sprinkle with hyssop or camphor oil. Invite people to stand and choose volunteers to wave the branches around as they walk up and down and sprinkle the fragranced water. Display the prayer for everyone to read aloud.

Heavenly Father

Thank you for purifying us through the blood of your Son, Jesus. Through him we are pure beyond words. Keep us clean, we pray. Amen.

Lord take away my sin and I will be so pure and clean
Wash me and I'll be whiter than the snow (x 2)

Whiter than the snow
Whiter than the snow
Whiter than a falling flake of snow

Lord take away my sin and I will be so pure and clean
Wash me and I'll be whiter than the snow.

Ian Smale

INCENSE

Malachi 1:11b

"My name will be great among the nations, from the rising to the setting of the sun. In every place incense and pure offerings will be brought to my name...."

Incense sticks; paper; pens.

The traditional way of using fragrance in a church is through burning incense. Incense is a symbol of our prayers rising up to the Lord. It is also symbolic of spiritual cleansing and has been used in Christian worship since early times. We see it commanded of the Jews (Exodus 30:1) and then used in worship in Israel from that point on. In the New Testament Zechariah offers incense in the sanctuary when the angel of the Lord appears to him (Luke 1:8–11). In Revelation the elders hold golden bowls of incense, 'which are the prayers of the saints' (Revelation 5:8). There are many different fragrances of incense. Try some out and see which one you like best. Make sure they are safely secured on a fireproof surface. As the incense burns, invite everyone to write or draw their own prayers with the words or pictures in 'smoke' rising like incense to God.

God commanded the use of incense in Jewish worship as a symbol of people's prayers rising up to him. It is still used for the same purpose in many Christian churches today. Certainly, using the sense of smell can help us to focus and concentrate our thoughts and words more powerfully. In advance, place incense sticks of various fragrances at random under chairs or seating. Invite those who find an incense stick to bring it to be lit. Light the incense sticks and display them safely on stands around your meeting place.

Father God

We join our worship with the saints who have gone before us, angels and heavenly beings around your throne and lift our hearts to you in prayer. May we always be the aroma of Christ, the fragrance of life, where we live and move and have our being. Amen.

May the peace and presence of the Lord
Fill our hearts and minds to overflowing
To keep our radiance showing
Keep our love for you growing

We pray this knowing
That as we walk in obedience
You give us all this and more
That as we walk in obedience
You give us all this and more

My Lord, my God, the firstborn of creation
The author and perfecter of my faith
My strength, my song, my captain of salvation,
Prince of Life, King of kings, God of grace.

Ian Smale

LEAVES

Revelation 22:1–2

Then the angel showed me the river of the water of life, as clear as crystal, flowing from the throne of God and of the Lamb down the middle of the great street of the city. On each side of the river stood the tree of life, bearing twelve crops of fruit, yielding its fruit every month. And the leaves of the tree are for the healing of the nations.

Leaves; paper; pens; paints; flowers; woodland-scented oil; pine oil; cedar wood and sandalwood bark chippings; large bowls; small plastic bags or fruit nets.

Collect a selection of different leaves from trees and invite everyone to identify them. Play a game to work out some names of trees whose leaves are said to have healing properties: Eucalyptus, Wintergreen, Holly, Balsam, Silver Birch, Walnut, Elder. Put dashes on the paper for each letter of the tree names, write in all vowels and put the other letters in a 'bank' at the bottom of the page. In Bible times, sometimes leaves were mixed with dried flowers and oil to make a perfumed mixture. Try mixing some small leaves and blossom flowers or dried flowers with a few drops of a woodland- or autumn-leaves-scented oil and breathe in its perfume.

In Bible times there were different methods for making fragrances. One used leaves and dried flowers mixed with perfumed oils. Some ingredients available then are still used today: cedar wood, cypress wood, incense, juniper, lavender, rose, cinnamon, marjoram and jasmine. Invite volunteers to concoct their own recipe for potpourri. Share the fragrances around for everyone to enjoy. Whose recipe smells best?

Lord, as we smell the mixture of the leaves and the oils, we pray that you will come with healing for our nation and for the rest of the world. Amen.

A little one shall become a thousand (x 3)
So says the Lord and in its time
I will do this swiftly

A little one shall be a mighty nation (x 3)
So says the Lord and in verse twenty-two
Of Isaiah sixty.

Ian Smale

LILY

Song of Solomon 2:1–2
I am a rose of Sharon, a lily of the valleys.

Blue cotton or silk; thread; needles; scissors; ribbon; rose petals or lily of the valley potpourri; paper; pens; frieze paper; card; paints; brushes; blue and green finger paints made from powder paint mixed with water and drops of floral oils.

The lily of the valley mentioned by Solomon was probably similar to the hyacinth and grew in fields and woods. These deep blue fragrant flowers cover the hills of Galilee in the spring. They are often used as a symbol for innocence, purity, wealth and power. Using blue cotton or silk fabric, make small scented bags of rose petals or potpourri scented with lily of the valley. Tie with a ribbon. Write out some different texts of encouragement, pop them in the bags and give them away to friends.

Choose volunteers to paint broad brush strokes on frieze paper, creating a wall mural of hills, trees and fields. Others, including children, can finger-paint blue flowers with green leaves for lily of the valley. As the mural is created, read out the various titles or names of Jesus. Jesus, the Name above all names, is all these, and more to us.

Lord, thank you for encouragement which is like a sweet smell full of fragrance and helps to make us feel valued. Amen.

May my praise be sung with feeling
May my worship be sincere
May my voice declare Jesus is God
For all the world to hear
May my mind be constantly renewed
May my thoughts be clean and pure
May my life be dedicated
To you whom I adore
I adore you, I adore you,
There's nothing I would rather do
Than simply adore you
I adore you, I adore you,
I want to live my whole life through
Simply adoring you.

Ian & Irene Smale

MINT

Luke 11:42

Woe to you Pharisees, because you give God a tenth of your mint, rue and all other kinds of garden herbs, but you neglect justice and the love of God. You should have practised the latter without leaving the former undone.

Ingredients for peppermint creams; fresh mint; mint sweets (made or bought); baskets; PowerPoint display.

Mint is mentioned only twice in the Bible and sadly when Jesus is rebuking the Pharisees. There were different varieties of mint used in the New Testament times. There was wild horsemint which grew on the banks and ditches of Palestine. Other mints were peppermint and pennyroyal mint. It was also used in medicinal remedies and in one ancient cookery book it is mentioned on every page. The Jews scattered mint on the floor of the synagogues so that the fragrance oozed out as they trod on it. Make peppermint creams from the recipe below. Children will find this recipe easy to make. You will need:

- 1 Egg White
- 450g Icing Sugar
- Peppermint Essence or Oil of Peppermint

Beat the egg white until frothy but not stiff. Sieve the icing sugar, adding enough to produce a fairly stiff mixture. Add a few drops of the essence or oil. Knead the mixture into a firm paste and roll on surface dusted with sieved icing sugar. Cut into rounds or form small balls and flatten. Place the peppermint creams onto parchment or silicon paper, place in a warm place to dry for 24 hours. Store in an airtight container or share out and enjoy.

Scatter mint leaves on the floor for people to walk across as they come into the room. Show a PowerPoint display of a variety of types of sweets (including mints). Conduct a poll to find the top three favourites. Even if not in the top three, mints are very popular. Mint has always been valuable, as the Pharisees well knew, and useful for medicinal, aromatic, culinary, household and decorative purposes. Today there are more than six hundred varieties of mint sweets – boiled with sugar is an enjoyable way to eat it. Pass around the mint sweets.

Dear Lord

Thank you for sweets we can smell, taste and enjoy. Please help us to be honest with you and one another and not to be like the Pharisees. Amen.

I don't want to be a Pharisee or anyone like that
It's stupid swallowing camels whilst straining at a gnat.
To keep the letter of the law,
They forgot the people it was for
So I don't want to be a Pharisee
I don't want to be a Pharisee
I don't want to be a Pharisee or anyone like that.

Ian Smale

MYRRH

Psalm 45:8

All your robes are fragrant with myrrh and aloes and cassia; from palaces adorned with ivory the music of the strings makes you glad.

Myrrh candle; paper; scented pens; digital camera; PowerPoint display.

Myrrh is a fragrant, sticky yellowish tree resin. Myrrh was brought to Jesus after his birth, offered to him on the cross and his body was anointed with it after his death. In Bible times it was used in medicine, cosmetics, perfume and oils for anointing and healing. One record shows an order for six hundred hin (over four thousand litres) of anointing oil for a gang of workmen. Invite everyone to draw pictures of family and friends or write their names on paper using the scented pens. Place the pictures and names in a circle and set a myrrh scented candle in the middle of the display. Now pray for each person as the scent of the myrrh fills the room.

With permission, take photos of people as they arrive and combine them into a PowerPoint display as the group time begins. In Bible times the tree from which myrrh was produced grew in Arabia. It is highly fragrant and it was an ingredient in the oil with which Aaron and his successors were anointed (Exodus 30:30). It was also used to perfume clothes and beds, in medicine and cosmetics, and mixed with frankincense to embalm the dead. This prophetic gift was given to Jesus as a child by the Magi. At his crucifixion myrrh was offered to Jesus mixed with wine to deaden his pain. Jesus refused it. Light a myrrh scented candle and invite everyone to pray for each other as the PowerPoint display is shown.

Heavenly Father

Thank you for my family and friends. Please help me to remember them in prayer before you. Amen.

Lord here we stand hand in hand
Praying together for every land
Ready and willing to obey your call
Caring and bringing your good news to all
Through loving others we hope and pray
That all will see Jesus is living today
Amen
Lord here we stand
Hand in hand

Ian & Irene Smale

IDEA 96

NARD

John 12:3

Then Mary took a pint of pure nard, an expensive perfume; she poured it on Jesus' feet and wiped his feet with her hair. And the house was filled with the fragrance of the perfume.

Peppermint, rosemary and thyme essential oils or shop-bought foot soak; bowls; towels; scented talcum powder; PowerPoint display.

Print out the texts below. Spikenard or nard as it is commonly called is a fragrant ointment made from a plant with scented roots. It is sometimes used to scent hair. In Bible times spikenard was imported from the Himalaya mountains in sealed alabaster boxes which were only opened on special occasions as it was very expensive. Give two options: children might like to draw round their feet, cut out the shapes and write or stick a pre-written Bible verse to them, and then drop a drop of oil on each paper foot (don't let essential oils touch skin directly). Adults may prefer to dust their feet with scented talcum powder. Read and repeat the texts and inhale the fragrance.

- Matthew 10:14: If anyone will not welcome you or listen to your words, shake the dust off your feet when you leave that home or town.
- John 13:5: After that, he poured water into a basin and began to wash his disciples' feet, drying them with the towel that was wrapped around him.
- Isaiah 52:7a: How beautiful on the mountains are the feet of those who bring good news.

Such a personal and public act of extravagant love was shocking to some. Mary anointed Jesus' feet with the most expensive and lavish expression she could think of. Nard was extremely expensive and reserved for very special occasions. How do we express our love for Jesus? In deeds of kindness? Service for him? Loving others? Seeking justice for those who have none? In the pressure of life it's good to stop and reflect on Jesus and our response to him. Set out bowls of warm water with a few drops of essential oils and invite volunteers to come and dip their feet. Display the verses as part of a PowerPoint display of the Himalayas.

Thank you Lord that you are more than generous to us. We do not deserve your love but you love us more than words can say.

How beautiful upon the mountains
Are the feet of those who bring
The happy news of peace and salvation
The news that the God of Israel reigns.

Ian Smale

PERFUME

Proverbs 27:9

Perfume and incense bring joy to the heart, and the pleasantness of one's friend springs from his earnest counsel.

Dried flower petals; matching essential oil; blank greetings cards; glue; cotton wool; plastic bags; flipchart and pen; flower-scented candles.

In Old Testament times kings and palaces all had their own perfumers as well as cooks and bakers. The perfumer's job was to supply not only the king with expensive oils and ointments but also the dignitaries and soldiers. Perfume was used in rituals, festivals and royal banquets. The perfumer was a type of cook and there were several techniques used to make perfume. Flowers were soaked in fat or dipped into hot fat or oils or they were pressed and squeezed in a bag. The scent of the flower was then mixed with the oil and strained leaving liquid perfume. There were also priests who were dedicated to make perfume and holy oil for the Tabernacle. Take some dried fragrant flower petals e.g. freesias or roses. Stick the petals onto a blank greeting card. Choose a matching fragrant oil and put a few drops onto some cotton wool. Place the card and the cotton wool into a plastic bag and seal for forty-eight hours. When you take the card out it should smell of the fragrant oil. Give the card to a friend.

Taste and smell are linked senses but smell is about ten thousand times more sensitive than taste. Smell receptors are found in the nasal cavity and when triggered by odours they send nerve impulses to the area of the brain involved with emotion and memory. That's why certain smells evoke a strong emotional and memory response. God is so creative! Invite everyone to list their favourite fragrance on the flipchart. Is there one that stands out as the most popular? Probably not. God has given us so many marvellous things to smell, each with their own unique perfume. Light the flower-scented candles as you pray and worship together.

Father God
Thank you for all the scents, perfumes and wonderful smells you have created to bring us joy. Amen.

I will sing,
I will always sing about the Lord's love (x 2)
I will say,
I will say your love will last forever (x 2)
Forever and ever
Amen.

Ian Smale

SCENTED LIGHT

Psalm 119:105

Your word is a lamp to my feet and a light for my path.

Air-hardening clay; string; matches; scented oils; various scented tea lights in glass votives; tables; lighters.

In Bible times lamps for domestic use were made out of bowls of oil, with strips of cloth to light which served as wicks. Sometimes they had a cover with a hole in the centre where the oil was poured in. The seven lamps of the golden lamp stand in the Tabernacle and the Temple were made of gold and burned with olive oil. In the fourth century Christian symbols like alpha, omega, a fish, a cross and a lamb were often moulded onto the lids of lamps. Today the Paschal candle usually has these symbols on it and it is lit in many churches to signify the presence of Christ as an illuminating light. Use air-hardening clay to mould a bowl-like receptacle with a lip at one side. Pour in a little scented oil and lay a small piece of string down the side of the lip into the oil to make a lamp.

Before people discovered gas and electricity and how to use them, lamps, candles and fire were the main means of light. The alternative was to go to bed when darkness fell and to get up when light returned. Light has always been important. For good reason Jesus is described as the Light of the World. Although we appreciate all the benefits of electricity many of us enjoy lamps and candlelight at home and church. The gentler light can aid our worship and prayer, and more so if fragrance is added. Place scented tea lights in glass votives on the floor to form a path shape. Invite everyone to come and light one of the tea lights or candles. Now turn out all the electric lights and as you follow the path of tea lights across the floor – pray.

Heavenly Father

Thank you for Jesus, light of the world, and for the fragrance of your lovely presence with us. Amen.

Arise shine for your light has come
And the glory of the Lord is upon you (x 2)
Arise shine for your light has come

So let's wake up with a noisy drum

So let's wake up with a guitar strum

So let's wake up with a cockerel's fun

Arise shine for your light has come
And the glory of the Lord,
The glory of the Lord
The glory of the Lord is upon you.

Ian Smale

IDEA 99

SOAP

Malachi 3:2b

He will be like a refiner's fire or a launderer's soap.

Bowls of water; towels; three muddy shirts; bars of household or launderer's soap, soap leaves; fragrant soaps; paper; scissors; paints; brushes.

The Hebrew word for soap is *borit*, meaning to purify. In Bible times soap was made by burning saltwort plants, of which the prickly saltwort was the most common. The ashes were rich in potash and were mixed with olive oil. The Arabic name for saltwort is *kali* and is where we get the word alkali from. The making of soap was an important trade in Palestine.

In advance, cut out some simple large paper clothes shapes e.g. socks, T-shirts, trousers, etc. Invite everyone to choose a paper clothes shape and a bar of soap. They should write, 'Jesus, wash me clean' on the paper using the edge of the soap like a crayon. Paint over the paper and it should reveal the words.

Set out six bowls of warm water on a table. Invite three volunteers to come and wash a muddy shirt with the launderer's soap. The shirts can be rubbed hard with the soap, releasing the scent, in one bowl and then rinsed in a second bowl. Squeeze them out well and hold them up. Are they clean? Not clean enough? Soap has long been used to clean clothes, homes and bodies. Malachi prophesied the Lord's coming to complete God's work in history and that when he comes he will cleanse like a refiner's fire or a launderer's soap. Give out soap leaves to take home as a reminder. Display the prayer. Stand and pray aloud together.

Dear Lord Jesus

Thank you that if we come to you and confess to you the wrong things that we have done, you forgive us and wash us clean. Amen.

God is here God is present
God is moving by his Spirit
Can you hear what he is saying
Are you willing to respond
God is here God is present
God is moving by his Spirit

Lord I open up my life to you
Please do just what you want.
Lord I won't stop loving you
You mean more to me than anything else.
Lord I won't stop loving you
You mean more to me than life itself.

Ian Smale

TABERNACLES

Leviticus 23:42–43

Live in booths for seven days: All native-born Israelites are to live in booths so that your descendants will know that I made the Israelites live in booths when I brought them out of Egypt. I am the Lord your God.

Citrus room sprays; citrus fruits; knife; glasses; water; ice cubes; paper; paints; containers.

The Feast of Tabernacles marked the end of the grape harvest. Tents would be constructed out of palm branches and children would decorate the tents with citrus fruits and wave the palm branches to signify the presence of God everywhere. They would live in these booths for seven days, surrounded by the smell of the freshly cut branches of palm, myrtle and wild olive trees. They would also have the fragrance of the citrus fruits. Squeeze grapefruit, lemon, orange and lime juice into green, yellow and orange paints. Paint green palm tents and then use lemons, limes and oranges cut in half to stamp yellow and orange fruits over the tents.

When the children of Israel celebrated the Feast of Tabernacles at the end of the grape harvest they lived for a week in tents or booths made of palm branches. They decorated the tents with citrus fruits. Throughout that time they inhaled the aromatic branches and the fruit, and enjoyed the presence of God. Spray citrus room sprays such as orange, lemon and grapefruit high up round the room. As the fragrance falls think about God and the fact that his presence is always with us.

Dear Lord

As the perfume fills this room please help me to draw closer to you. Amen.

Blessed is the King who comes in the name of the Lord
Blessed is the King who comes in the name of the Lord

Peace in heaven and glory in the highest
When mouths stay closed the stones will cry out
Peace in heaven and glory in the highest
When mouths stay closed the stones will cry out

Majestic is the King who comes in the name of the Lord (x 2)

Triumphant is the King who comes in the name of the Lord (x 2)

Ian Smale

Bible Index

Numbers refer to ideas, not to pages.